I0569288

Margaret (Marjori) Wiese

The
Bee
Tree

Primix Publishing
East Brunswick Office Evolution
1 Tower Center Boulevard, Ste 1510
East Brunswick, NJ 08816
www.primixpublishing.com
Phone: 1-800-538-5788

ISBN: 979-8-89194-199-1(sc)
ISBN: 979-8-89194-200-4(e)

Library of Congress Control Number: 2024911226

Published by Primix Publishing: 02/13/2025

PRIMIX
PUBLISHING
THE WRITE CHOICE

Dedication

This book is dedicated to Abba Father, Jesus, and Holy Spirit! And to Margaret Wiese's family and friends. Those people along the way that encouraged her to keep writing and to one day be known as a great author.

Photo by Margene Wiese-Baier

Contents

Prelude

The Pacific Northwest

*I*n the Pacific Northwest, autumn rains imparity to the long hot summer. The nights are cool and frisky. Fall winds nip gently, almost caressingly, hinting of the winter months to come. The rain falls, lightly at first, then with tempo, starts a pitter-pattering on the rooftops like a lullaby. Sometimes, the sun heralds a day of warmth. On these sunny days, the red-winged blackbird flits from fence post to fence post; mostly, it just sits there, head cocked and listening.

The rain may continue for days, but there are intervals when the full moon casts its haunting glow on deep forested glens, snow-crested mountains, and shimmering stars.

In October—late October, that is—there is a chill in the air. Most of the orchard-grown fruits have been harvested. Squirrels chatter and scamper from tree to tree pleased with their winter hoard of nuts and cones. Many birds join in the bustle, their songs loud and lacking the melodious tones of spring.

Part I
The Hiltons
October 1962

Chapter 1

John and Nell

As John Hilton drove into the driveway, he saw his wife, Nell, by the pear tree. She was picking up the windfalls and throwing them into a box. The bees were swarming angrily around her head, but she was so intent on her task that she seemed to be unaware of the bees.

"Nell, I'm home," John shouted as he took the newspaper from the porch and walked into the house. Seconds later, Nell appeared beside him.

"When did you get home? I was so mad about the mess those pears are making on the lawn, I didn't see you drive up. John, I want you to go over to the Wrights. Tell them to pick their rotten pears or I'll cut the damn tree down."

John tossed the paper in a chair, then he grabbed at her.

"Know something? You're sexy when you're mad."

The phone rang. Nell drew away from him and hurried to the kitchen to answer the call. John picked up the paper, quickly flipping to the sports section. He continued to read until dinner was ready.

"Where's the twins?" John asked, as if they were one instead of two as he sat down at the table.

"Where?" Nell echoed. "God only knows. I think Jean is visiting a friend and Jess called to say she's stopping by the library."

John thought of the twins, born minutes apart, but different as night and day. He missed them running to him the minute he walked through the door, but they were teenagers now, not the little girls he often wished they were.

"When do those kids eat?' he asked.

Nell did not reply. He sat impatiently, watching her complete the small chores of the evening meal. Communication had become a major problem.

"Know what I remember most about my mother?" he said. Nell looked at him, questioning. "No, what?" John thought for a moment before answering.

"We were home at mealtime. We sat down at the dinner table together. You're too damned easy on those kids."

Nell felt an inclination to say, "Well, why don't you have a talk with them? You're their father." But she didn't.

Why start an argument? she thought.

"Did Rob write?" John asked, trying to start a conversation.

Nell shook her head. John finished eating in silence, his thoughts privately condemning himself for the way he neglected the children. He was spending more time at the office, seeing less of the twins when they probably needed him the most. Rob was away at college. The years had gone by so swiftly that now he could not remember Rob as ever being a little boy.

Nell poured the coffee, and John noted her dinner had consisted of coffee and fruit. Another diet— she was always on one diet or starting another.

"I like my women well stacked," he had told her one time when she was complaining about her weight. The thought forced a smile on his face.

"What's so funny? See Mrs. Rice today? She called right after you left for the office."

At Mrs. Rice's name, John winced. "Why'd you have to mention her name? Any aspirin? I've got one hell of a headache."

Nell massaged the back of his neck.

"You're so tense, why don't you lie down? I'll bring you some aspirin and a glass of water."

John felt disturbed and angry. Mentally, he rehashed the conversation with Mrs. Rice. Selling insurance to Mrs. Rice was like being in the ring; she blocked every punch.

"Mr. Hilton, Tom and I are insurance poor," she said, her voice more shrill with each sentence. "Tom took out a twenty-five-hundred-dollar policy five years ago. I'm sure when it's his time to go, it'll bury him."

John's head was splitting.

"I'm sure it would be, Mrs. Rice, but with Social Security the way it is and your daughter nearly ready for college, how would you manage?"

He closed his eyes. *How in the world can some-body like that get me into such a foul mood?* Nell brought in the aspirin and a glass of water and tip-toed quietly out the door.

In his dream, the pear tree grew in a vast desert.

Cold winds tore at the sand, raking in great black clouds, separating him from Nell.

"Nell," he called. She did not reply. He knew she was beside the pear tree because there was a mon-ster of a beehive and Nell was the queen. "Nell," he shouted again.

Awakened by a soft tap on the door, he realized he had been dreaming.

His bed was wet with perspiration, and there was a strange prickly sensation on the back of his neck.

"What's the matter, Daddy? Having a nightmare? You were calling for Mom."

It was Jean.

John rose from the bed and quickly ran a comb through his hair. He had a nightmare.

"Oh, I was just wondering, where is your mother?"

"She's cleaning up the kitchen. By the way, Daddy, I've got to have fourteen dollars," she added coyly, "for cheerleader outfits."

John reached for his billfold.

"Ye gads, you kids bleed me. Who the heck do you think I am? Rockefeller?" He fumbled with a twenty-dollar bill, then teasingly withdrew his hand. "What happened to the five bucks I gave you Monday?"

He started to tell her about the nights he worked to put himself through college, but she interrupted him.

"I know, Daddy, but jobs were easier to get in the old days. All there is now is babysitting and housecleaning."

"Well, then how about helping your mother? And why can't you get home in time for dinner?"

Jean appeared bruised. John seldom scolded her; it wasn't like him at all.

"Daddy," she pleaded. "Can I have the money?"

Surprised to see the bill in his hand, he handed her the money. He just couldn't say no; maybe giving them what they wanted was his way of making it up to them for not being home more often.

"Thanks," she said, planting a kiss on his forehead, then paused, running her fingers across his head. "Your hair's sure getting thin on top."

For a moment, he had the impulse to strike her. Today had brought one blow after another. *Someone has to remind me that I'm getting bald.*

The next morning, John's desk was stacked with the usual insurance paraphernalia: policies to be signed and the mounting number of complaints had become a daily chore.

He had not slept well the night before and he still had a vile headache. *Nine-thirty,* he thought, glancing at his watch. *Nine-thirty and I'm already beat.* His secretary Valerie brought him a cup of coffee. He put the papers to the side of the desk, shoved his chair back, and sat staring into space, grappling with what seemed to him a hopeless situation.

At ten o'clock, he was still sitting in the same position. Valerie put the morning mail on the desk.

"Mr. Hilton, there's a brochure about the sales conference in Seattle, shall I call for reservations?"

"Wow, three days from now, that's cutting it close. The old man's a stickler on these things, better call right away." He fumbled through the papers on his desk, then rummaged through the files.

"If you're looking for the Nelson files, I have them. You wanted a duplicate."

"Get them, Valerie," he said under his breath. "I'm sorry, Mr. Hilton. I didn't hear you."

It suddenly occurred to him he didn't want her to hear. At the moment, he didn't give a damn about the Nelson files.

"It wasn't important, but you better call the airport, and there's some motels listed in the brochure."

There were times during the war when days away from Nell grew into weeks, months, then years. This time, it would be only a few days, three days to be exact. Something nagged at him. He had to talk to Nell. Valerie was still on the phone, and he paced impatiently back and forth, waiting for her to finish the call.

When the phone was free, he dialed his home phone number, thumping his fingers on the desk. The phone rang, five, ten times. *Where in hell is she?* he thought. The phone rang a few more times, and he slammed the receiver down and rushed out the door. The abrupt departure left Valerie aghast.

"Night," she called after him, shrugging her shoulders when she realized it wasn't even lunchtime. "Wonder what's bugging him," she said to herself.

Nell was sitting at her desk, writing a letter.

"Can't you answer the damned phone?" John said, walking up behind her.

She looked at him, startled. "Home early, aren't you?" Suddenly, John wondered why he was so angry.

"I left some papers in another suit," he lied. "Who's the letter to?" he said, peering over her shoulder.

"David Wright, Harry's brother." Nell read the letter to him.

Dear Mr. Wright,

Your brother Harry gave me your address and suggested I write you. It seems the fruit is not picked from the pear tree and falls on our side of the fence.

We have recently planted a new lawn and are unable to care for it properly with the leaves and fruit continually falling on it.

Harry said I would need your permission to have the tree removed.

"Think that's OK?" she said, then licked the envelope flap and pressed it down securely. "Sounds dumb, having to get permission to get rid of that old tree. It's about ready to fall down anyway."

John did not answer her. Driving back to the office, he fought nausea. Nell worrying over a stupid tree. If she doesn't quit spending money like it's free, she'll have something to worry about!

Monday morning, the alarm rang. John felt as if he had spent an entire night awake. The smell of perking coffee and bacon sizzling stimulated his appetite, and he groped for his robe, stretched a few times, and waited in line at the bathroom. Nell had laid out his blue suit and red tie. *Something's wrong,* he thought as he shaved. Things weren't going as planned, neither at home nor at the office.

"Losing your grip, old man?" he asked his reflection, patched his nicked chin, and cursed Nell under his breath for shaving her legs with his razor. Breakfast on the table but his appetite had vanished.

He picked at the eggs, then glanced at his watch.

"Better beat it, don't want to miss the plane."

He put his suit coat on and picked up his luggage. Tears were starting to well in Nell's eyes.

"Heh! I haven't left yet." He tipped her chin and kissed her quickly on the lips.

Nell rubbed at her eyes with the back of her hand. "Will you miss me?" she asked, searching his eyes.

"I'll call every night," he promised as he rushed out the door. "Be good!"

"Be good!" Nell echoed. "What about you? You'll be in Seattle with all those other wolves and I'll be stuck here with nothing but housework and a messy yard. We never do anything together anymore."

John hesitated. "You had your chance last night. Remember?"

He had ripped the fancy trimmings off the sore spot in their relationship. Nell watched as he drove away, feeling as if a cloud of moths were fluttering inside her.

Chapter 2
Nell's Transformation

The morning passed so slowly for Nell; by midafternoon, she felt lonely and afraid. *I hate being by myself.* The book she had been reading the night before was nowhere in sight.

John's been angry with me all week, she mused. *I don't even know why. Oh, yes, the book.*

She spotted the book on the nightstand, but she walked past it. Taking her coat from the closet, she tossed it over her shoulders and walked swiftly out to the garage.

The air was crisp, and she shivered. *Winter again. Spring is gone, summer is gone, and autumn's gone. Everything is going somewhere, and I'm going to pot.* She started the Lincoln and headed toward town.

The beauty shop was at the end of Third Street. It irritated Nell that parking was so inadequate, and she drove around the block looking for a parking space. She found a parking space. She found a spot behind a large semi-truck near a seedy-looking café.

Once, she had patronized the most elite shop in town; now she looked for an obscure one, hoping she would not be recognized. Everything irritated her lately. The girl at the reception desk seemed too absorbed in a true-confessions magazine to look up. When she did notice Nell, she asked, "Can I help you?" in what Nell thought was a disinterested tone.

"I'd like a shampoo and set—facial, too," Nell added, noticing another woman relaxing while the cosmetician massaged her face. Soothing.

"Nancy," the receptionist called to someone unseen from the front desk. "A lady wants her hair done."

Nell's hair was brushed briskly, then shampooed vigorously. Nell appreciated that! She had been so tense lately, and it seemed to release the built-up tension. While her hair was wound on oversized rollers, she talked casually with the hairdresser. *This is just what I needed. I haven't been out of the house in a week. I can't believe just having my hair done can feel so good.*

She was being draped, creamed, and massaged. A beauty mask brushed delicately over the cleansed skin. She riffled through the pages of a fashion magazine while the mask hardened and her hair dried. With each page turned, she felt older, worse, fat, ugly fat.

"You know, Mrs. Hilton, you'd be a young-looking woman if you didn't have those crow's feet around your eyes. As soon as we get this off, I'll demonstrate a new wrinkle remover, it's not permanent, but it lasts for several hours" was the sales pitch.

Cold fluid was applied gently around Nell's eyes. As it contacted the skin, Nell could feel the tightness.

"Want to see yourself?" the girl asked, handing Nell a small round hand mirror.

It was true. The lines were barely noticeable. Nell bought the wrinkle remover, paid for her beauty services at the front desk, then hurried back to the cosmetic counter where she picked out a pale shade of lipstick. She glanced in the mirrors on her way out to the door. Her reflection startled her. She did look younger, but still matronly. Her sunglasses were in her purse, and she put them on and rushed out to her car. The children should be home, and if they weren't…she suddenly felt angry.

It was nearly five-thirty when Nell turned into the driveway. The sky was pink and gray. *Like marble,* she thought. It's getting dark so early. She locked the garage door and took the newspaper into the house.

There was a scribbled note from Jean, propped among the dirty dishes.

"We'll be home about ten," it said, not bothering to mention where they were going.

Nell stacked the dishes into the dishwasher, wiped the table, and then poured herself a cup of stale coffee and sat by the kitchen table reading the newspaper. Quickly scanning the headlines, then turned to the want ads.

Maybe someday she'd go back to work. Someday, when the twins were graduated. As usual, there was nothing that interested her in the ads. Everyone wanted someone with experience—well, she was experienced: twenty-two years of housework, yard work, taking care of children, and picking up after John.

She folded the newspaper carelessly and took it into the living room and dropped it on the coffee table. She glanced up at the picture of her mother on the fireplace mantle. Aloud, she said, "Mother, you said that the older you became, the happier you were. You said that age mellowed you and made life easier to handle. It's a lie! A damned lie!"

As soon as she had said that, she regretted it. Her mother had been dead for six years and never had Nell called her a liar.

The photo still stared at her from the mantle, and she took the picture down and placed it face down on the couch.

"I'm sorry, Mother," she said, placing the picture back in its place. "Honestly, I am."

The silence was haunting her, so she put a record on the stereo. When the music blared forth, she sat down on the rug, raising her arms above her head, rocking on her buttocks back and forth across the floor. "One, two, three," she counted. Perspiring, she continued her calisthenics until she was exhausted. Then for no apparent reason, she began to cry.

John had suggested that these periodical crying jags were due to the change. Now the thought of his saying that made her furious. After going through a regular sobbing ritual, she looked at herself in the mirror.

Her face was rosy, and her skin looked young and vibrant. Though tears, her mascara smeared and ran down her cheeks, in the soft shadows of dusk, the telltale signs of age had vanished.

"It's true," she whispered. "You're only as old as you feel." She flung her sweater over her shoulders and ran out the door.

The fruit was gone from the pear tree, and the leaves lay crisp beneath her feet. The monotonous buzzing of the bees was the only sound she heard. As she leaned against the fence, the pear tree held a strange fascination to her: she was a little girl again; her mother was holding her close, soothing away her fears.

"Mama," Nell wept. But she was alone with only the stars above her and the same wind blew against her face that shook the straggly branches of the old tree.

"I wanted you destroyed," she crooned. "But you're like me. Nothing will topple you, not the rain, the wind, nor age, you need to have birds nesting in your branches and bees buzzing around you—I need someone, too."

The dampened air had relaxed the set in her hair and it caressed her shoulders. She felt the wind grow cold blew through her thin clothing. The wet grass swished against her bare legs. Like an agile child, she climbed over the fence into the Wright's yard and stood next to the pear tree.

The bees buzzed angrily, intuitively noting a strangeness. Momentarily, the humming ceased. The Wright's dogs were barking. Nell heard the continuous whir of the cars pass on the highway, and she shivered at the frightful cry of a night bird. Dead twigs snapped and a shadowy form came toward her.

"What are you doing out here?" a male voice demanded. "You some kind of a nut?"

He was a stranger to Nell.

"I just went for a walk," she said, embarrassed.

The man stood very near her, so close that she could feel the warmth of his body.

Animal heat! she thought.

"It was a nice night," she stammered, attempting an explanation. "I'm David, Harry's brother, you're Nell Hilton, aren't you?"

"Yes," she said, barely audible, "I just wrote you, you couldn't have gotten my letter yet. I sent it to Pennsylvania."

"Letter? I came down from Seattle to visit Harry. I've been stuck up there for a year, so I thought as long as I was that close, I'd visit him before I have to go home. He told me you were peeved about the old tree, the pears making a mess on your lawn and all that."

David Wright put his hand on the tree as if to balance his stance. "I know this sounds crazy, superstitious even, but old Silas would turn over in his grave if anything happened to it. He was my great-grandfather, planted that tree way back in 1879. Yeah." He scratched his head with his other hand, and Nell sensed a smile in his voice. "He was a funny old duck, all right, even wrote it down in the Bible. Something about life having no end, you know, immortality that sort of thing." He paused, waiting for Nell to speak, but she seemed hypnotized. "And I asked if you were a nut," he said.

"Did you bring your family?" Nell asked quickly, trying to steer him from the subject.

"No, I came alone—divorced," he ended the sentence, "moved up from California. Old Pete Larson's. It's crowded there, and we used to farm the old home place, but Jen, that was my wife, hated it. Too far from her family."

"I'm sorry she didn't like it," Nell said meekly.

"It sure is being built up around here. The old Larson house used to sit right there." He pointed to the left, although it was too dark for Nell to determine just where the house had been. "There was no fence then. Harry said you folks move awful. I like it here, but it's lonely. I haven't met many of my neighbors yet."

"Won't be that way for long. Some big outfit bought the land right down the road, going to put in a big housing development. I've got to get back," she said, starting to walk away.

In the darkness, she stumbled. He drew her gently to her feet. In the excitement, his grasp tightened and Nell pressed against him. He was a complete stranger, yet she felt that he had been part of her for all eternity. Calmly and deliberately, she cast convention to the winds.

Nell crept silently into the house. She undressed quickly and slipped into bed. Only when dawn aroused the birds and daylight filtered through the cracks in the blinds did she stir. For one revealing moment, the truth existed.

I'm Nell Hilton, she thought, *married to John. We've shared our bed for more than twenty years.* She turned over and went back to sleep, dreaming the same dream over again.

A man was chasing her around the pear tree. She was very young—seventeen or eighteen. The man almost caught her, and she was throbbing with the thrill of the chase. The bees swarmed down, and he ran from her. When Nell awakened, she was angry.

Still shaking from anger, she raised the window shade, letting it slap the top of the window. Her hairbrush was lying on the nightstand; she brushed her hair, piling it high on her head in juvenile abandon, letting it fall on her bared shoulders. Suddenly, she no longer felt gay. *What got into me?* she questioned. *A wife, a mother. Well, I don't give a damn! They don't need me.* Frantic little thoughts clamored for attention. *Now I know what's wrong with me. Sex—in big capital letters. SEX!*

Nauseated, she rushed to the bathroom. *I used to get sick to my stomach when Mother lectured me about boys. Mother is dead, but I haven't changed! Mother is still punishing me.* She examined her thoughts ruthlessly. *Oh, it's not Mother punishing me. It's me, Nell Hilton, and I'm punishing myself.*

Chapter 3
John meeting Marla

Oh, God, why did John have to go to Seattle now of all times?

It rained most of the time John was in Seattle. The motel was close to the conference hall, and he ate breakfast at the coffee shop, where he had been introduced to Marla Henderson, one of the few women attending the convention. She seemed shy at first but accepted his invitation to lunch. Now he wondered if she would come at all, she was ten minutes late.

John saw Marla Henderson walk through the door—the tan belted raincoat, a lavender scarf confining the pale blonde hair.

His eyes met hers just as she walked through the door. He experienced the same emotional impact he had when they first met.

"Heavens, John?" she said when they were introduced. "We don't have many women salesmen in the insurance business."

He wished he would have said something, but she smiled and agreed to have lunch with him. Now he sat across the table from her and he still couldn't think of anything to say. The lunch hour was almost over; the café empty of garbled discussions. John reached for her hand.

Marla met his gaze steadily. "I'd like that, might break the monotony. Some of those speakers are surely long-winded."

John glanced nervously at his watch. "We're late. It's after one. See you this evening then?"

She quickly scribbled her address on a piece of paper from her notebook and pressed it into his hand.

"It's a date," she said.

Back in the motel, John took the address from his pocket, memorized it, and crumpled it up in a little ball and put it back into his pocket. *This could happen to Rob,* he thought. *But it's happening to me, his old man.* His tie felt uncomfortable, and he took it off along with his shoes and socks.

Slumping in a chair, he kept imagining how it would feel to touch her. She looked so soft and her perfume doing things to him. There was a vague yearning; like remembering something special, only now he couldn't get it together. Soft and responsive.

Responsive, that's the right word. The scent of her returned to his memory.

"It's a date," she had said, and the way she said it held promise.

The torrential rains had turned to showers when John parked the rental car in front of Marla's apartment. She did.

"Have dinner with me tonight?" he asked. "We could see a movie afterward."

His tie felt uncomfortable, and he took it off. There was no answer to the doorbell, and he felt panicky, frantic with the fear he had been stood up.

He pounded on the door persistently, then stood back ready to leave when Marla opened the door.

"Oh," she said, "I forgot to tell you that the doorbell is broken—I put a note up, must have blown away." She held the door open. "Come in, I'll be ready in a minute."

Her dress was a soft blue, and the round necklace reminded him of one of Nell's, a moment of remorse for asking her out. Looking into her eyes, the thought of Nell was fleeting. Damn her eyes! Blue green or green with blue specks, a mole on her chin, right where I'd touch if I'd tip her chin to kiss her. A beauty mark, not a disfigurement.

"Would you like a drink?" she asked, hesitating, fearful he might get the wrong impression of her.

"Sounds good to me."

"Make yourself at home," she called from the kitchen where he heard the clinking of glass and ice. She handed him the drink and sat on the divan across from him. "Is it all right, the drink? I don't have much experience bartending."

"It's fine, hits the spot." For a moment, he seemed to be lost for words. It hadn't occurred to him that she was shy; now it seemed he would have to steer the conversation. "Where are you from originally? You have sort of an accent."

Marla laughed. "I have? I'm from Wisconsin, you know the state of the big cheeses."

The reply was meant to be humorous, but John had missed the point while mentally pursuing other interests.

"Aren't you going to have one with me?" he asked, raising the glass to his lips.

"I don't drink. My father was a minister. I guess that will stick with me all my life."

"I respect you for that, I really do," John said, helping her with her coat.

Over dinner, John heard himself talking end-lessly, saying one thing while he was thinking another. "Marla, that's a strange name, but somehow you look like a Marla."

Nell doesn't want me. She doesn't want anyone else to want me either. He ordered a martini, drank that, and ordered another one. The more he drank, the more he imagined that Marla looked like the girl he had met for the first time. She had been blonde also, soft blonde with the bluest eyes. Memories flicked before him. "Honey," the girl had said at the dance, "let's get some fresh air."

Reliving the semi-successful episode, his early triumph brought back the old youthful excitement. Only it wasn't Geraldine, it was a beautiful blonde, a real lady, and he was making headway.

Or was he? Maybe he was making an ass of himself.

Nell always said he made an ass of himself when he drank too much.

"John," the lady across from him was saying.

For a moment, he had to force his mind to concentrate on just where he was and with whom.

"John," she repeated, "do you like the insurance business?"

John looked at her, pondering the question. "Sometimes it's a rat race, you know how it is? High pressuring, just to put food in the kid's mouth. Like little birds," he laughed, "their mouths are always open." He patted her hand as if she was one of the twins. "Sorry, honey, I'm monopolizing." The word was difficult to pronounce.

"Heh, I'm doing all the talking. You tell me about you. I want to know all there is about you."

"There's not much to tell. I'm a widow. I have a son in college. My husband was killed in the South Pacific."

John looked at her sadly. "I'm sorry about that." He reached out and touched her hair. "Is that real? I mean the natural color. Now you're mad at me for asking such personal questions."

"I don't mind. It's really blonde, dishwater blonde. I lighten now."

"I like it! Looks real nice and soft. My wife wouldn't look nice blonde. Her eyes are dark—you should see when she's pissed off at me. They spit fire."

At the mention of his wife, he could feel Marla grew more tense.

"Don't get me wrong. I'm not one of those guys that rims down his wife. Right now, no one can live with her, going through the change. I don't blame her for that, I guess most women get like that. I've tried to get her to go to a doctor, but she won't go, thinks she isn't old enough."

Marla glanced toward the clock. "It's getting late. I'd better take a rain check on the movie."

Driving back to Marla's place, John was apologetic.

"I didn't mean to embarrass you. I usually don't drink that much. I wanted to show you a nice time."

"I had a nice time. I enjoyed talking to you."

When John walked her to the door, he kissed her gently, then stepped back as if he expected a rejection. He had almost forgotten how passionate a kiss could make one feel.

"Can I come in?" he asked huskily.

There was a childish urgency in his request and Marla weakened.

"I guess it would be all right," she said softly.

It was strange to be in another woman's apartment. There had been that time overseas, but that was when he was younger.

It was different than being with Nell, always that wall between them. Now he didn't have a care; he was just a man preparing in his mind all the things he would say to the woman he was trying to seduce.

For Marla, it was as if life were starting over again.

She found John easy to talk to and wanted to tell him everything about her life. She really wanted him to know her understand her.

"When Frank was killed, I didn't want to live," she told him. "I couldn't focus on anything. It was as if I were two different people— one wanting to live, the other wanting to die. I didn't know which one would win. I was trying to raise Steve alone. I was working at a defense plant and I'd be so tired at night, sometimes I thought I would just drop.

"Sometimes, I think we have guardian angels, like those my father used to preach about. I'd get so depressed sometimes that I felt like ending it all.

"I even thought I was going crazy, looking for a way to kill myself, like slashing my wrists or taking some pills. But do you know what happened when I felt like that? Steve, he was only a baby then, about three 'cause he could talk. He'd sit on my lap when I was crying and hug me, and I guess I knew I had to take care of him."

She started to cry, and John held her in his arms.

"Go ahead and cry, honey, sometimes we just have to let go."

She was still sobbing. "He didn't even see his father, but he always talked about him like he did. He'd always ask if I didn't love Daddy anymore, just like he knew. I've got to tell you something, John," she said. "You might not want to hear it, but I've got to tell you."

"Nothing you could tell me would change the way I feel about you."

"I had therapy, you know, I was mixed up. Dr. Morrie made me see how morbid it was to hang on to the past. Frank was dead, I was alive. I had to think about Steve. I learned something I won't ever forget though, life is for living, you've got to take the bad right along with the good. If you draw the wrong card, you still have to play it."

At that moment, John felt a paternal urge to protect her, yet he felt possessive and jealous of anyone who may have been as close to her as he felt right now.

"Have you—has there been many men since Frank?"

"I don't know what you mean," she stammered, a delicate flush suffusing her face. "I date sometimes. I'm not promiscuous, if that's what you mean. I was just a kid when I married Frank."

She looked away from him, nervously fingering some magazines on the table.

He kissed her, trying to block out the implications of his statement. "It doesn't matter, honey. I didn't mean anything by it. I'm jealous."

"John," she said wistfully, her eyes meeting his, "Why do men think women feel different about sex and things? Something is missing in your life or you wouldn't be here. Something's wrong with my life or I wouldn't allow you to be here. Sometimes it happens like that other. Is it so awful to need someone?"

The invitation was free of all pretense, her hand gently escorting him into the bedroom. John took it and closed the door.

Chapter 4

Nell daydreams about David Wright

At six o'clock Tuesday evening, Nell opened a can of tomato soup, made cheeseburgers, and poured the milk. With John away, it seemed useless to prepare a big meal.

The twins ate their supper and left for the young people's meeting at the church. The moment they slammed the door, Nell felt panicky. A home once bursting with activity seemed unfamiliar—like a tomb, John had once said.

She quickly cleared the table, put the dishes in the dishwasher, and reread the evening news. An hour had passed. Maybe she'd have her bath and go to bed early and read. She went into the bathroom and poured bath oil and bubble bath into the tub, turning the faucets on full force. While the water ran, she perched by the stereo until her favorite record ended, then mixed herself a drink. Every record played seemed to be her personally. Her and David Wright.

When she returned to the bathroom, bubbles were climbing the pink-tiled wall. She giggled. Dropping her clothes in a heap on the floor, she sank into the fragrant water. Only her shower-capped head and her hand holding the drink remained above the bubbles. Every time she closed her eyes, she could see David, hear his voice, feels his hands…thoughts going through her mind.

All day she had kept busy, polishing silver, dusting, and finally sorting the records in Rob's room. The violin sat in the comer, and as much as she had nagged, Rob had given up his lessons. *Playboy* magazines were still strewn on the nightstand. How upset she had been when she found Rob goggling over the centerfolds. How it seemed so ludicrous, Rob had become a man.

Then the phone rang, she rushed to answer it— angry because the call was for John. She had peered out of the window, hoping for a glimpse of David; a lovesick schoolgirl, she had waited in despair.

A day's so long, I wish the kids were babies again: diapers, formulas, colic, I wouldn't have time to think.

Stepping from the tub, she dried her body with the twin's beach towel and reached for the bottle of wrinkle remover, sprinkled a few drops on a cotton ball, and placed it around her eyes and the corners of her mouths—wherever an unwanted line existed.

Powdered and flower fresh, she slipped into red nylon pajamas and her silk Chinese duster.

"Just where do you think you're going?" she asked herself while brushing the set from her hair.

Another twenty minutes squandered in the bathroom. Time is something you never have enough, then a day comes like this. *I could spend all night fixing up—for whom?*

Rummaging through the nail polishes, she chose a pale pink. *If I put on red, the twins will question my sanity.* It took several more minutes for her fingernails to dry. The soiled clothing lay in a heap on the bathroom floor; she picked them up and tossed the bundle into the washing machine.

She poured another drink; she slithered into the family room and sat in John's recliner. Bored, she turned the television on and sipped at her drink. The Chinese lanterns used for the September dinner party were still hanging from the beams. She lit the candle, then sat back down again, watching until it burned out. The room was chilly, and she went out to the patio to get some wood for the fireplace. The fire blazed and she sat back down again and closed her eyes.

The night of the party she had tried to be a good hostess. *I wanted to make an impression on John, I helped him. That night, he even kissed me differently, not the husband-wife peck, but a long sensual one. I went to bed and waited for John. When he did come to bed, he had drank too much, it was just awful…another big disappointment.*

The fire was almost burned out, and she went back out to the patio to get some more wood. There was a full moon, and its glow shone like sparks on the dew clinging to the shrubbery. In the house again, she laid the wood carefully on the fire and mixed herself another drink. *I've always learned the hard way,* she thought, *women give their hearts and souls to love. Men love for love's sake alone.* She had read that somewhere.

There was a tapping on the back door. *The wind,* she thought. The tapping continued. She sat her drink down on the table John had recently refinished, then picked the glass up quickly lest it leave a ring. She set the glass on the bar and went to the door.

David Wright stood in the doorway.

"I was going to call, but thought it would be better to apologize to you in person. I'm sorry about last night."

"There was nothing to apologize for. We're both adults." She held the door open. "Come in, I'm alone tonight."

"I don't want to make a pest of myself," he said, stepping inside,

"I'm glad you came. I wanted you to come."

Soft lights haloed her hair; it looked as fluorescent and shiny as a raven's wing. She looked young! She was young! For a fleeting moment, she was aware of life—life that stagnates only when love is gone.

Later, she lay awake. *I'm even with John now,* she thought. But it was not joy she felt. It was a fierce agony. Each night has a million stars, and though dark clouds hide them from view, they are still there. As many stars as there are in the sky, people live their lives— tears, laughter, unfaithfulness, true love, and barren love. "Oh, God," she wept, "is anyone really happy?"

Nell crept from her bed to the window. In the Wright's house, lights flickered off one by one. *David,* she thought, or any man, anyone who would have come to the house tonight. She drew

47

the window shade down as far as it would go and reached for her drink in the darkness. Things were not clear in her mind anymore and she was still alone. Desperately alone…

Chapter 5

Rob deciding to go home for a Visit

Rob Hilton slammed his books down on his study table, then walked out onto the campus. His hands in his pockets, he watched the students hurry to and fro, holding hands, laughing and talking. He kicked viciously at an apple core and sent the wasps flying. In his confusion, he started to whistle in an effort to forget his misery. His mother had her heart set on him being a lawyer following her father's and great-grandfather's profession. *She'll have a fit,* he thought, *when she finds out I flunked my term paper.*

The apple core and the wasps kept nagging at him, reminding him of the Wright's pear tree and the bees. He felt in his pocket for some loose change and found a phone booth and called his mother.

"Rob," Nell's voice bubbled with anticipation. Then sensing that something was amiss, she said, "Are you all right? I was thinking about you, you didn't write."

"I'm OK. I just wanted to let you know I'm coming home next weekend. Is it all right if I bring a girl?"

"Pat Martin?"

"No, a foreign student. Her name's Lottie—she's real cool. You'll like her, Mom."

"What happened to Pat Martin? She seemed to be a very nice girl."

"Oh, I don't know. See you Friday night, about seven or eight."

"Drive carefully. The roads are bad. Rob, I'll have dinner waiting, so don't stop and eat."

"OK. Bye, Mom. Say hi to Dad and the brats."

"They wouldn't appreciate your calling them that." "I'm just feeling ornery."

Rob waited a few moments, wondering how to tell her.

Well, he just wasn't a brain. "Bye," he said again, dropping the receiver quietly into the cradle.

Lottie shyly avoided Rob's eyes as he slipped into the chair next to her.

"Hi, Lottie."

She raised her eyes slowly. "Oh, hi, Rob."

A born flirt, he thought, and that wasn't all. He glanced at Pat Martin and wondered why he had lost interest. A virgin, brains and looks—a rare commodity on the campus. Pat felt Rob's eyes on her, and she playfully wrinkled her nose at him.

The professor dismissed the class. Rob lingered near Lottie while she chatted with some other girls. When he saw the group breaking up, he moved in.

"I just talked to my mother. She invited you for the weekend."

Lottie's ebony eyes beamed.

"Oh, Rob, how nice."

"Everything's OK then? Be ready right after English Comp. I'll pick you up at the dorm." He started to walk away, then called to her. "Bring any old thing to knock around in. We live in the boondocks."

Lottie laughed. "Really, you kidding?"

Rob lowered the top of his sports car, watching the wind whip Lottie's black hair. A doll, he thought, almond eyes, a widow's peak that makes her face a perfect heart shape, cute nose. Her hair caught the sun's rays, and he couldn't keep his mind off her.

"You're a flower, Lottie."

"You making fun of my name?"

"No, I wasn't. I think you're lovely. Like a lotus flower."

"Thank you, Rob, always you say nice things." She snuggled closer to him. Looking up at him, she slipped her arm around his waist. The hairs on his arms bristled when he felt her warm breath against his neck.

"Light me a cig, will you, honey?" he said, pushing the lighter in. He brought his hand back and let it rest on her bare knee. She reached into his shirt pocket, took out a cigarette, put it carefully between her lips, lit it, then placed it into his mouth.

Gad, he thought, *she's even sexy when she's lighting a cigarette.*

"Smoke?" he asked her.

"No, I do not smoke. It is not attractive for women to smoke."

"Bravo! I agree with you. My mother doesn't smoke either."

"You are very fond of your mother?" she asked, looking at him intently.

Rob withdrew the cigarette abruptly from his lips.

"Yes," he said quietly, as if she had discovered one of his dark, hidden secrets.

The sun began to sink behind the foothills. There was a sharp curve in the road and the bright rays shone directly into Rob's eyes.

"See if my sunglasses are in the glove box," he said to Lottie, fighting to keep the car on the road.

Lottie fumbled among the maps and oddments. "No, there are no glasses."

"Must have left them in Pete's Sprite," he said, steering the car toward the graveled shoulder.

"Why did we stop?" Lottie asked anxiously.

"Too damn dangerous! The curves are the devil. No sense taking chances."

Rob drove the car into a narrow side road and cut the motor. He shoved the seat back as far as it would go, then reached for Lottie, drawing her close against him. She pushed him from her when he slipped his hand under her sweater.

"Rob, not before I meet your mother."

He reached for her again. "I'm not going to rape you. Can't a guy get a kiss without getting shoved through the windshield?"

"Please, Rob," she pleaded. "Always before you were gentle, this time you frighten me."

"You've got me riled, you know that, don't you?" he said, stroking her bare arms, the nape of her neck, and then the soft flesh of her inner thighs. "I'll be gentle," so stirred, he could scarcely breathe. "I swear I will."

"It is different here," Lottie said, surrendering. "In my country, we love only after marriage. Here, it is some kind of a game, everyone counting how many times you can do it all in one night."

The sun now completely veiled by the gathering evening mist, a madness seemed to seize him. Lottie was silent but for the deep breaths that seemed synchronized with his. Her skin was as smooth as the petals of a flower and a peace emerged over him.

Later, back on the highway, she sat quietly beside him. "I am very wicked."

"No, Lottie, you were wonderful, we'll stop at a service station so you can wash up and fix your hair."

Lottie put her hand to her head. "Oh, Rob, I look that bad?" She drew away from his side, sitting far to the right.

"Rob, you did not use those things."

Rob did not reply. The rest of the trip, not a word passed between them.

It was nearly nine o'clock when they reached the Hiltons. Nell met them at the door.

"Mom," Rob said. "This is Lottie, I can't pronounce her last name."

"Kwang Su," Lottie said, holding out her hand to Nell.

Nell hesitated, then took her hand. "I'm happy to meet you, Lottie. Find a chair, dinner's in the oven," she said, going into the kitchen.

"Where's Dad?" Rob asked.

Nell called from the kitchen, "He's changing a tire."

Minutes later, John soon appeared in a pair of overalls.

"I'll be with you kids in a minute," he said, walking past them to change.

After dinner, they went into the family room and sat before the fire.

"Rob says you're an exchange student," John said suddenly.

"I come from Korea," Lottie said proudly.

Nell rose quickly from her chair. "May I be excused? I don't feel well."

John looked at Nell critically, forcing his cigarette out in the ashtray. "Can I get you something?"

"No," Nell said apologetically. "I'll be all right, one of those dizzy spells again."

Nell left the room just when the twins and their teenaged friends barged through the door. They rushed past Rob and Lottie.

"Girls," John said. "Get in here and pay your respects to your brother and his friend."

"Oh, hi, Rob," Jean said. "I didn't know you were coming."

They both looked at Lottie. "It's nice to meet you. Where's Mom?' they asked, running the sentences together.

"She's lying down," John said quickly. "Eat your dinner and get to the dishes."

"We don't have time," Jess said. "We've got to decorate for the hop. Mom doesn't do a thing all day, let her do it."

"The dishes!" John said angrily.

The twins exchanged bewildered looks, then Jean pleaded, "Daddy, do we have to?"

"You have to," John said firmly.

"We'll see you later," Jean said to her friends at the door. "Daddy must have got up on the wrong side of the bed."

"Hop to those dishes!" John shouted at them again.

"We heard you the first time," Jess yelled back

"OK. OK. We heard you the first time. You don't have to holler."

"I could just see my mouth if I'd have talked back like that," Rob said to Lottie.

Lottie sat restless. "Rob, it is wrong that I come. Please, we go back tonight."

Rob squeezed her hand. "Don't be silly, hon, we're just a nutty family. Mom has those spells all the time. As for the brats, they're brainless."

"I want to go back."

"I didn't drive all that way just to turn right around and go back," Rob said firmly.

Lottie hated any implication that she was different. *White,* she thought, *the superior race subject to the same frailties as any other race. The haughty mother, impolite teenagers, everyone making me feel inferior.* She wanted to find somewhere she could be alone and cry.

"Excuse me, Rob," she said. "I go and help in the kitchen."

John moved his chair closer to Rob, his voice barely audible above the chatter of the girls in the kitchen.

"How's school? Lottie seems like a nice girl," he added without waiting for an answer to his first question.

"Wish Mom thought so."

John cleared his throat. "'Well, there's nothing serious between you, is there?"

Rob looked at his father, confused by such directness.

"I've dated her a few times—sure, I like her. She's really something. Know what I mean?"

John got up from his chair and went to the portable bar. "Drink?" he asked Rob.

"No thanks," Rob said, wishing he dared to have one. He remembered one time when he was about twelve, maybe even older; his dad had caught him smoking and made him inhale. He had felt very grown up dragging in on the cigarette, then almost choked to death while his dad watched him.

John sat back down, balancing his drink on the arm of the chair. "Then it is serious?"

"What's serious?" Rob had forgotten just where the conversation had been interrupted.

"This thing with Lottie."

"Hell, Dad, I didn't say that."

John took a drink, then sat it back down again. He took his pipe from his pocket and filled it with tobacco, nervously pressing the tobacco into the bowl.

"Son," he said, wrestling with a match. "It's my fault your mother is upset over Lottie. Remember, I spent a couple years in Japan. Occupation." John tapped the pipe against the fireplace brick, knocking the unsmoked tobacco into the fire.

"You see, I met this Japanese woman. We lived together, shacked up, the old army lingo puts it." He took another drink. "Don't get me wrong, I'm not making excuses. The war was over. It's just not easy telling you your old man wasn't true blue and all that."

"Then why are you telling me?"

"I don't know. Maybe to keep you from making the same mistakes I did."

"And you told Mom?"

"No," John refilled the pipe, lit it, and puffed a couple times. "No, I didn't tell her. Women have intuitions, and I'll be damned if they don't always hit it right on the head."

"But she never rode you about it—not in front of us kids anyway."

"No, maybe she didn't. But she punishes me for it every minute of every day."

"Your conscience bothering you, Dad?"

"Hell no!" John got up and poured another drink. "Hitting the bottle a little hard, aren't you?"

John set the glass down quickly. "I have a few now and then. It gets pretty hectic at the office and your mother never quits griping."

After he said that, he felt like a liar. Nell never talked much when she was angry with him, she usually clammed up.

"Damn it!" Rob said. "I wish I'd have brought Pat Martin instead." At that moment, he felt as if he were the father and John the son.

"I've been one hell of an example." John paused. "There's a lot more to breaking moral codes than what meets the eye. You pay for it in more ways than one. You can't cheat without paying a price and another woman doesn't erase it from your mind."

Now his father sounded a little drunk. Voice of experience! Rob wanted to shout. Instead he said, "You're telling me the facts of life a little late, aren't you?"

John who had seemed so staunch now looked weak and old and outdated, laying his soul bare before his son.

"Damn this whole f——ing world," Rob cursed as he watched his dad pour another drink, then Rob walked down the hallway to his mother's bedroom.

Nell was sitting on the edge of the bed, fumbling with her handkerchief when Rob came into the room.

"I was just going to powder my nose," she said.

"You should see a doctor, it could be something serious."

"I'm all right. At my age, I've got to expect some changes."

Rob sat down beside her. "I shouldn't have brought Lottie this weekend. I didn't know you weren't feeling well."

"I didn't mean to be rude, Rob, you have to believe that."

"You and Dad scrapping again?"

"No, it's not that. Things have been bothering me—I don't even know what."

"I'm just sorry I brought Lottie, that's all." "It wasn't Lottie, honestly."

"Mom, I know you've been lonely. I even know how you felt when Dad was overseas. Don't you think it would be the same here if Russia or Red China attacked us? Do you think all the girls would remain virtuous? It's plain psychology: women are attracted to the opposite, the stronger side, and, Mom, face facts, men are weaker sexually."

"Then you condone your father's tom-catting around, even what he did in Japan?"

"I don't know what he did in Japan." Rob was on a merry-go-round, overreacting, trying to protect his father. "I can't judge him, Mom, him or anyone else. I don't even know what I'd do if I were in Vietnam, even if I were married."

Nell looked at Rob. "Let's drop it, just drop it."

Rob was no longer a child; he no longer depended on her judgments.

"I like Lottie, it doesn't make one damn bit of difference to me what color she is. We have students from Africa, too, they're blacker than the ace of spades. You're lucky I didn't bring one of them home with me."

"You're accusing me of prejudice." "You said it, I didn't."

Nell rose from the bed and stood before her dressing table.

"It's your life, Rob. As for Lottie, I'd think about it a bit before I got involved."

"For god's sake, Mom, you're making a mountain out of a molehill. I should have brought Pat Martin. She's more to your liking, isn't she? Of course it has nothing to do with the fact her old man's worth a mint."

Nell laid her hairbrush on the table. *Is this Rob?* she thought. *Is this how I appear to him?*

"Rob, please. That's not true."

"It's just that I can't picture you prejudiced, you always seemed to be so damned broadminded."

"I'm not prejudiced. It's a difficult world without creating more problems." She slipped her shoes on, then looked carefully at Rob. "I'll be out in a minute, have your dad put on some fresh coffee."

Rob put his arm around his mother. "Don't worry, Mom, I'm going to stay a bachelor and make 'em all happy."

"Rob," she said softly. "Tell Lottie, explain to Lottie. I wasn't angry about her coming, it wasn't that."

Chapter 6

Rob and Lottie

Rob had not spoken to Lottie for over a month since the weekend with his parents. He felt that she didn't want to see him. Perhaps, if he were honest with himself, he would have realized that it was the other way around. He had deliberately avoided her.

"Rob, we must talk." There was an urgent tug at his sleeve.

"Oh, hi, Lottie, long time no see. I tried calling you," he lied. "What's new?"

"We cannot talk here. Maybe we go for a ride."

"Sure, doll. Anywhere special?"

"No place special, somewhere we can be alone."

"I'll drop these books off at the library. Pick you up around about seven. OK?"

It had started to rain, and Lottie was waiting on the steps of the dorm when he drove up. She was wearing a red and white scarf tied snugly beneath her chin. She did not see him drive up, so he pressed hard on the horn trying to draw her attention.

Lottie smiled when she recognized him, but looked ashamed when he continued honking.

"Get in," he shouted to her.

Lottie got into the seat beside him.

"It is wet," she said, dabbing at the droplets on her face. "Where to?" he asked without looking at her. "Just drive. I am out of breath, we talk later."

They had driven around a few blocks when Rob glanced toward her. "I wanted to see you, Lottie. Honest. I was just too ashamed. I don't know what the heck got into my folks."

"They are not used to my ways," she said, folding her scarf neatly and tucking it into her handbag. "It is not your mother that upsets me so."

"Is it me? Something I did?"

She clasped and unclasped her hands, tears seeping from her eyes.

"Bad as that?" He started to laugh at her smudged makeup. "Somebody die or something?"

"You will be angry at me."

"How can I be mad at you? I don't even know what you're bawling about."

"Rob, I don't know how to say it." She made a circular motion over her abdomen. "I am pregnant—that's how you say it?"

Rob clutched the steering wheel with both hands. Shocked and surprised, he drew the car to a stop in a private driveway.

"Is that your idea of a joke?"

She started to sob. "I'm frightened. I cannot go home now. You promised I would not get a baby."

"That's plain stupid, how dumb can you be?"

"It was only with you. Always you used one of those things. Last time you did not."

"Have you been to a doctor?"

"I do not need a doctor." She lifted her hands in a gesture of hopelessness. "Always it come one time a month, like a clock. Just this one time I miss."

Rob sighed in relief. "It could be the flu, maybe female trouble, maybe your imagination."

"It is not imagination. Already I feel morning sick."

"Listen, Lottie, let's not get shook up until we know for sure." "You would marry me?"

"I couldn't marry you. I couldn't support a wife and go to school too."

"It is that you do not love me."

"Love?" He spoke the word as if it were foreign and he didn't know its meaning. "What has love got to do with it? It's the principle of the thing."

"Now, I do not want marriage with you. Take me home!"

He started the motor and reeled out. When he stopped in front of the dorm, he held her in his arms for a moment, the old emotion making him blind to his promises. "I like you a lot, Lottie. I'm just not ready. Promise me you'll go to a doctor."

Lottie got out of the car and walked slowly up the steps. She did not look back as he drove away.

It was one o'clock in the morning when Rob called his father. The phone rang repeatedly before John answered it.

"Hello, hello," John's sleepy voice finally responded. For a moment, Rob did not speak. He almost hung up the receiver, then realized it would be a dirty trick to hang up after he got his dad out of bed.

"Dad, this is Rob, is Mom asleep?" he said in almost a whisper. "Can you talk louder? It is Rob, isn't it?"

"I'll get right to the point, Dad, but I don't want Mom to know I called."

"Shoot. Your mother's asleep. She had a head-ache and went to bed early."

"Remember Lottie, Dad? She thinks she's pregnant." "What?" John shouted.

"Think I should marry her?"

"Are you damned sure you're responsible?" "Yes," Rob said quietly.

"It won't be a picnic telling your mother you knocked some dame up."

Rob felt nauseated. "Dad, do you always have to be so crude? Well, I'm waiting, what should I do?" He felt like a little boy begging his father not to spank him because he had been naughty.

"Nothing. First find out if she's really pregnant." "She said she's sure. She never missed before.

He heard his father curse. "Tell her to go to a doctor. Don't jump into anything, Rob, are you still there?"

Rob did not answer. He plopped the receiver into the cradle, cutting off the chill of his father's voice.

It took Rob a long time to get to sleep. In his tormented state, he kept dozing off, then awakening with a start. When he did sleep, he had a very vivid dream.

It was a beautiful wedding. All of his relatives from California were there. Lottie was dressed in magnificent white, and her skin looked like pure ivory. White and lavender orchids with yellow throats were suspended from the chandeliers, dancing gently as the breezes caressed them. John sat in the front pew and the twins sat next to him. He searched the crowd for his mother, but he couldn't see her.

The ceremony ended, and he and Lottie rushed out across a vast lawn and reached the waiting car. But it wasn't a car; it was a coffin, and his mother lay there with her hands folded over her chest. The casket was piled with flowers, ferns, ribbons, leaves, and petals that covered her body. He awakened with a sob.

Not the grown Rob, but the little boy of five who had cried all night when his mother was in the hospital having the twins, believing, knowing that he would never see her again.

When Rob really awakened, the sun was peering lazily through the window. The phone was ringing, and he wrestled, untangling the cord before he could answer it. The dean wanted to see him.

Rob tapped lightly on the door of the dean's office. "Come in."

"You wanted to see me, sir?" Rob asked boldly, trying to mask his fear.

"Sit down, Rob." Dean Lewis looked stern behind the thick rimmed glasses. "Thought you might be able to help us." The dean studied Rob. "It seems Lotus Kwang Su plans to drop out next term." The dean flipped through some papers in his hand. "She's a good student, very good."

"I know Lottie."

"You've been dating her for some time, haven't you?" "I've taken her out, nothing steady."

The dean sat back in his chair, rubbing at his chin.

"Do you know if she has any problems at home or…?" "No, sir," Rob lied.

Dean Lewis took his glasses and wiped them with his handkerchief. Piercing blue eyes peered into Rob's. "That will be all. Thought you might be able to give us a clue."

"No, sir, I can't," Rob said, getting up quickly.

Rob walked past the library and saw Pat Martin sitting alone, almost as if she had been waiting for him. She smiled, and he sat down beside her. Without speaking a word to him, she took his hand and held it between her own.

Chapter 7
Rob and Pat Martin getting Married

Nell Hilton half dried her hands on her apron, seeing the mailman stop at the mailbox. There was the daily junk, and she felt jubilant when she found a letter from Rob.

His letters had been few and far between, as had his phone calls since she had been so rude to Lottie. As usual, his handwriting was small and barely legible. It was a brief note, and she felt shortchanged.

"Pat Martin and I will be married on Friday afternoon. We plan on stopping by on our way to the coast. Short honeymoon, heh? See you then."

Nell folded the letter and stuck it in her apron pocket. Pat Martin? Only a short time ago, it had been Lottie. She had thought Rob was in love with Lottie. Was he ready for marriage? *Twenty-one, impulsive like his father,* she thought. *Well, I hope he knows what he's doing. How can he support a wife? It's hard enough scraping up tuition.*

She wanted him to be a lawyer, but he changed his major to political science or something like that. She sighed. Why was it so hard to see your children mature and marry? She poured a cup of coffee and sat cross-legged on the divan. The house was a mess, but she felt too numb to clean it up. She let the coffee get cold while trying to call John's office. He was out.

When she went out into the kitchen to make fresh coffee, the wind was whipping the shrubbery against the window, and it was raining. John had asked her to take in the patio furniture and she rushed outside. She folded the lounge and chairs and lugged them up the ladder to the garage rafters. The gate was swinging wildly back and forth on the hinges, and she fastened the latch, then hurried back toward the house. Black clouds hung low over the trees. The air had a peculiar odor, and she felt a foreboding premonition of disaster.

Inside again, she rushed from room to room, turning on the lights. A fire was blazing brightly in the fireplace, and she stood before it warming herself. Away from the fire, she felt cold and put a sweater over her long-sleeved blouse.

Still shivering, she poured another cup of coffee and peered out of the window. The clouds were directly overhead, and she was certain that she heard a rumble of thunder. It rarely thundered, and she remembered having the same scared feeling when she was a little girl. Whenever thunder and lightning appeared, her mother had taken her down into a dark cellar.

Now she watched from the window as the velocity of the wind increased, playing havoc with oak trees in the pasture across the road. Clusters of leaves were torn from the branches and sucked into a whirlwind; higher and higher, they spun until they disappeared. Branches flew from trees as if torn off by a giant hand, leaving ragged and mutilated strips of bark and slivered wood. *It isn't happening,* Nell thought, viewing the storm as if it were a scene on television.

The back door flew open, and Nell shoved against the door, forcing the latch. Something sailed past the window. The patio roof had been torn off. She watched its flight until it crashed into the Wright's field. Phone and electric wires twisted in front of the window. Lights flickered for several moments, then went out. She tried the light switch! Dead.

The phone was dead, and she was frantic when she could not get through to John. The sliding glass doors bowed in, and somewhere, she heard the sound of breaking glass. Without thinking of the consequences, she unlatched the kitchen door and ran across the lawn toward the Wright's. Their old barn lay in a shambles and the trees in the orchard had been uprooted, stripped of branches and covered with muck.

She had not thought of the pear tree until she found herself beneath it. That was indestructible like her mother, she thought. But it stood like a nude statue, barren of branches or leaves. There was no sign of the bees; instinct had forewarned them of the approaching cataclysm. Nell clutched at the bark of the tree; windswept branches beat against her, knocking her to the ground. Sobbing, she kept clinging to the tree. A siren screamed as an ambulance speeded past on the highway; horns honking and a steady flow of traffic moved down the highway. Rising to her feet, she realized the winds had stopped. The storm was over.

Drenched and weary, she wondered how long she had been out there, and she picked her way back to the house, cautiously avoiding fallen wires and debris. Her garden looked as if someone had beaten the flowers with a switch. Then she saw it. Not more than ten feet away from the old pear tree was another tree, four or five feet tall. It must have been there for a long time, she thought, the shrubbery hiding it until now. The old tree had to die to make room for it.

Mother had to die, so I could grow and live. Someday, I'll have to die to make room for my grandchildren. Each generation is but the seed that lives on.

What a stupid thing to do, she thought, when she was warm and safe in the house. *I could have been killed.* The kitchen clock had stopped at 3:15, the time the electricity went off. She had left her watch in the bathroom, and she was shocked to see it was already past six.

The house was dark, and she took the flashlight to candles. Rummaging through the hall closet, she found an old kerosene lamp. It had some kerosene in it, and she lit it, appreciating the pale glow. Where in the world was John? The twins? Rob? In her own danger, she had almost forgotten about them.

"Please, God," she prayed. "Don't let anything happen to them."

The phone was out so she knew not to expect a call.

She tried to keep busy to maintain her sanity. The chalk squeaked and she felt like screaming when she wrote a note to herself on the kitchen blackboard.

Change bedding, dust furniture, vacuum. Vacuum, she rubbed the word off with the heel of her hand. In big letters, she printed: FIX DINNER.

"To hell with it!" she said, realizing she could do very little without electricity. She scribbled over the other reminders, chills creeping over her, shuddering, her fingernail scraped over the board.

Rob was coming home and he was bringing Pat Martin. They were married. Nell started to weep, then went into Rob's room, trying to make it presentable for Rob's wife. Rob's wife. Put feminine touches to a masculine room—orange and tan plaid bedspread, thick cotton draperies, travel posters, the stack of *Playboy* magazines. Tearing off the bedding from the bed, she felt a terrible emptiness, like losing something.

After her mother died, Nell had stored the bedding in the cedar chest. *Mama liked pretty things, I always tried to make her comfortable when she visited me. I loved Mama—I really did.* The pale pink sheets and satin comforter made the bed look feminine. Just making the bed that way transformed Rob's room into something that was not Rob.

This bedspread did not match the draperies, and it bothered her until she remembered the white Pricillas she had taken down from the dining room. She had stored them where? The hall closet— everything in the hall closet. She found the curtains and dug out some of her old paintings. *Not bad, Nell Hilton, you could have been a great artist.* She laughed. *Not great, but good. Even Professor Einhart had said so. But time has a way of revealing whether one's talents are real or imaginary.*

Well, I had a great imagination.

After the curtains were put up and the paintings replaced the travel posters, she stood back admiring her work.

Looks sharp in the lamplight, she decided, but how will it look in real light? Real lights, what's real and what isn't?

She stacked the magazines in the vacant place in the closet, then back to Rob's room.

"What in the heck's going on?" John stood in the doorway.

"Where have you been?" she demanded, forgetting the storm, then seeing John drenched to the skin and exhausted, she quickly changed her tone. "I've been worried sick about you."

"Came in the back way. I got six miles the other side of Johnson Creek, hiked the rest of the way. A big fir fell right in front of me— scared the hell out of me." He reached for her, holding her to him for a moment.

Nell returned his kiss. "I imagined all kinds of things, the girls? Oh, John, Rob's married." She started to cry. "Rob and Pat Martin are married."

"Hey, slow down. First, the girls are OK. They're staying in town. How, what about Rob?"

"He's married."

"Why the heck are you bawling? You knew that someday sooner or later he'd find a girl and get married." He handed Nell a soggy handkerchief. "Blow your nose and get me something to eat. I'm starved."

"The electricity's off, you'll have to have a sandwich and milk. I can't cook."

"All the way home I thought about having a cup of steaming coffee and a thick steak. I have to settle for a glass of milk and a sandwich. Is that how you treat a guy who walked through a storm to get home to you? That's gratitude!"

Tears streamed down Nell's face. John looked at her, tipping her chin, searching her eyes. "Honey, I was only kidding."

Later, they sat in front of the fire, Nell resting her head on John's shoulder.

"This is really the beginning, isn't it? The kids will be gone, there'll just be the two of us. Until today, I never thought I could stand the loneliness, then suddenly I realized, right in the middle of the storm, I've missed a lot, maybe ten years, maybe all the years we've been married. Time just went on by, I wasn't really living."

She was being silly, well, it didn't matter. John was fast asleep, and she was only talking to herself.

John eased himself into a comfortable position, as Nell placed a pillow beneath his head and covered him with the afghan she had made. John had walked all that way; he could have stopped somewhere, but he had worried about her being alone. She sat watching him sleep. She was sleepy too, but she couldn't sleep. She felt so guilty, wallowing in self-pity, not appreciating John when he worked long hours just so she and the children could have all the comforts. All these years she had not forgiven him, he had made one mistake. Was she so lily-white herself?

How simple, she thought, *it is to forgive—let bygones be bygones.*

It was nearly midnight when John awakened Nell, trying to guide her into their room.

"Unbutton me, will you?" she said sleepily, turning so he could reach the buttons down the back of her blouse.

Warm fingers fumbled with her undergarments and she felt a glow, almost like their wedding night.

"Put my robe on the bed in case there's another storm," she said and crept beneath the covers.

Nell had slept for several hours when she awakened with a start. Rob and Pat had not come in. She mentally timed their trip, and they were long overdue. She got out of bed and put on her robe. There were coals in the fireplace, and she put some wood on it. Moonlight was shining through the windows, and the night looked quiet and peaceful as if there never was a storm.

But shadows danced against the walls like monstrous demons, and she felt safety only near John. She went back to bed, lying close to him. She could feel his heart beating steadily. Her heart beat was fast and erratic. *Fear does strange things,* she thought. *I guess I've been afraid of something all my life.*

Sleep should come easily. They say that sex is a great reliever of tension. It was good tonight.

Kaleidoscopic thoughts. I know now why my mother always protected me and always wanted the best for me. And I know why I was afraid of her. Afraid of my mother? How did that thought creep in?

She tried to remember the relationship. Daddy died and left Mother alone. *I was their only child. Then I was so busy with my own family that I neglected her. She died alone in that big house. That's why I'm afraid too. But why couldn't I see it before? Mother was happy in that house, she said so lots of times. It's the way I'll be. There will be memories and all the little things that make a family. Like the way I felt when I was getting Rob's room ready for his bride.*

Mother had her own friends and her hobbies. She kept busy. It was really what she wanted. She kept telling me so, but I wouldn't believe it.

She was sleeping soundly when she was awakened by a loud pounding on the door

"Let the kids in," she murmured to John, slipping on her robe and brushing her hair. It was almost daylight and she was surprised she had slept that long.

"Hungry?" she asked, hugging Rob. She smiled at Pat and put her cheek against her face. "It was a surprise, but I wish you all the happiness in the world."

"We ate at the coffee shop on the peak. Boy, did we have a blast, finally followed a power crew. We're beat—hope the bed's ready."

"I changed a few things around," Nell said, "so Pat would be more comfortable."

Rob kissed her. "Night, Mom, hope you won't mind us hitting the sack right away.

"Good night, Mrs. Hilton, Mr. Hilton," Pat called they closed door of their room.

"Your folks are sure dolls," Pat said seriously. "Gee, this room is neat. Your mother has good taste."

"You should have seen it before. Boy, did I have the crap tacked up. Say, Mom's a pretty good artist, isn't she?" he commented, noticing the painting above the bed. It was a mountain scene, but it reminded him of another painting: of a Geisha girl arranging flowers.

He caressed Pat, running his fingers through her short sandy hair, but when he closed his eyes, the girl next to him had jet-black hair, almond eyes, and a cute little nose.

"Love me?" Pat murmured, nestling in the circle of his arms.

He kissed her on the throat. "Of course, silly. Do I have to prove it to you?"

"Prove it," she whispered huskily.

He lay close to her and her soft breathing aroused him, but as yet, he could not fulfill his marital obligations. He'd wait until sleep and weariness fogged his mind, and he could imagine she was Lottie. *Oh, God,* he wondered, *will this pain ever go away?*

Chapter 8
Nell going to Church

Nell entered the church for Sunday morning services. It was almost filled to capacity. There was a seat near the pastor's wife and children, but today, Nell did not feel that pure. She meekly followed the usher to a seat near the door.

The lilies on the altar seemed symbolic. They were as white as snow. Nell felt as red as blood. The minister, Nell noted, had a round, almost angelic face with serious, solemn eyes. It was a kind, strong face, not handsome but showed character. To her, he looked like God.

The congregation rose and sang, "Saved by the blood. Saved! Saved, my sins are all pardoned, my guilt is all gone! Saved. I am saved by the blood of the crucified One!"

Nell's hand clutched her hymnal as she bowed her head in the prayer that followed. It was a direct plea for Christ to deliver the sinner. Only through

His grace would all transgressions be stricken from the record. Nell glanced toward the center section, where the twins sat and smiled.

They smiled back, and Nell dug her fingernails into her palms. She had sat in church countless times during the past several years. It had become a habit—a status symbol, John had once reminded her. Church membership was good for business.

Nell had almost given up Sunday worship; it seemed impossible that she could again find God's grace. She had sinned. Could Christ dispel the shadow?

"Our text for today," the pastor intoned, "is found in the King James version, the sixth chapter of Romans, verse twenty-three: For the wages of sin is death; but the gift of God is eternal life through Jesus Christ our Lord."

He closed the Bible and scanned the faces of the congregation. From Nell's position, the people all looked alike. *What are their lives like?* she wondered. *Is there anyone else in this whole church that feels as I do?*

"All have sinned and fall short of the Glory of God," the minister began. "Indeed, not only every one of you but your shepherd as well. Yes, I am but human, with all the frailties of my sheep. I, too, have sinned. Doesn't that make you feel wonderful? We are all brethren held together by a common bond. Friends, there was but One man on earth who lived a sin-free life, the Lord Jesus Christ.

"In the Epistle of Paul, the Apostle, to the Romans, it is written, Therefore, being justified by faith, we have peace with God through our Lord Jesus Christ.

"According to Paul, we are justified by faith—freed from the law, not free to break that law. For in Christ's own words, that law is not destroyed. Think not that I am come to destroy the law or the prophets: I am not come to destroy, but to fulfill. For verily I say unto you, till heaven and earth pass, one jot or one title shall in no wise pass from the law till all be fulfilled.

"God set forth His commandments on a table of stone to Moses. That has not been destroyed. God never changes. He expects as much of us today as He did when He led Moses through the wilderness.

"But I never steal and I have never murdered. Thou shalt not, that is about all the commandments mean to us today and so we break the law helter-skelter, as if it did not exist.

"The first commandment states, Thou shalt have no other gods before me. There is but one God, no Christian will argue that point, but there are some in our world today who are willing to believe that there is no God at all or that God is dead. Some may even hint that God is some kind of a king sitting on a throne high in the sky, shaking his finger warningly when something wrong is done.

"But I am speaking of the living God. No other has the power to forgive, to make you again white and pure, though you are stained with sin." His voice quivered.

Nell swallowed and clasped her hands tightly in her lap.

"Yet how many of you grieve our Father by worshipping an image? An image just as despicable as the golden calf.

"It is not a sin to desire things of comfort. There is an abundance and that is good. Share His Kingdom and His promises. You will be showered with so many blessings, you will not have room for them all.

"Let us get the right perspective on money. It is merely a medium of exchange, not the root of all evil. But a love of money, to esteem money above all else, is to worship an idol.

"Thou shall not take the name of the Lord Thy God in vain. In vain, to use His name as a curse, to damn this and that. His name is sacred, it is blessed. We can call upon it in every trouble. It is ours to use in prayer and in praise. If God were but an earthly father, would He not turn from us when we curse Him? But He is all powerful. He is ever faithful. Though we turn our back on Him, He never turns His face from us.

"Today is Sunday, a holy day, a day of rest. Through the ages, history and tradition have made it so. It is a day to meditate, to give thanks! It is also a great day for joyrides, fishing, mowing the lawn, or having the relatives over for a big dinner. Is this wrong? Christ healed on Sunday. We must be guided by the whispers of our soul. Is it good? Is it for Christ? Do we return to our jobs on Monday renewed and rested, or do we start the new week exhausted by our Sunday activities?

"Thou shalt honor thy father and thy mother that it may be well with thee and thou mayest live long on the earth. Children, do you love your mother and father? Do you daily bless the paths that they have trod for you? How many of you—I include adults with aged parents—did not at one time think your parents somewhat stupid?

"Oh, yes, the younger generation! My dear parents, have you deserved the love you expect your children to give you? How often do we expect our children to attain goals we ourselves have been unable to attain? Yet we are but mirrors of our children, and our children are but reflections of us.

"My friends, I would not be in the pulpit today except by the Grace of God. I had a mother and a father who, when told of my intention to enter the ministry, helped me through the darkest perils. They stood by me while I wrestled and searched. They guided me yet gave me a free rein. So it is with our heavenly Father. He guides us, but we are free to choose our own way. His way leads to happiness untold, our way can lead to death and misery.

"Thou shalt not kill. This is a harsh commandment for we kill in many ways. Whenever we destroy or limit the talents God has given us, when we criticize instead of praising, we murder the desires within the heart."

The congregation was silent. A cough or the cry of a child did not rate the usual turned head. Nell's heart was pounding. The next commandment forbade her private sin.

"The next commandment is often glossed over by ministers. Thou shalt not commit adultery. The penalty of the Old Testament was death. It is still death."

Nell shivered.

"It is still death," he repeated, "but there is redemption. Did not Christ say to the sinful woman, 'Go and sin no more'? Sex is the image of today. My friends, we are being brainwashed by the advertising media—sex to sell cigarettes, liquor, clothes. But, my friends, it goes beyond that! You are being lured into purchasing automobiles, soaps, foods, cosmetics, and medicines by the same means.

"If you so much as look upon a woman and lust after her in your heart, you have committed adultery. Don't look at your neighbor, my friend. Do not cast that first stone. All are guilty, yet all is not lost. Though we be as red as blood, we can be as pure as the first snow. Humble yourself before the Lamb and He will sustain you. He will wipe away your tears.

"Thou shalt not steal. This commandment has been broken by those of us who would not dream of taking a penny that did not belong to us. There are many ways of stealing besides bank robbery, purse snatching, shoplifting, cheating on your income tax. There is dishonesty in business, selling for an exorbitant price, dispensing inferior goods, falsifying advertising, pilfering an employer of goods or time. Worldly goods may be stolen, so it is with spiritual goods.

"It seems that God has built a mountain of do's and don'ts. Do unto others as you do unto yourselves. You would not rob yourself, you would not bear false witness against the one you love the most. We should fear and love God, respect Our Creator, and obey His commandments. We should not lie, betray, slander, or defame our neighbor. We should not covet our neighbor's house or anything that is our neighbor's. We should not think of ways to beat our neighbor out of what is rightfully his. And we have the infinite power of prayer.

"The only formula for prayer to God is to ask. Ask in faith, ask in truth, and be sure you want what you ask for. Have the faith to trust and thank God that we do not always receive what we ask because sometimes we do not ask wisely.

"Your very thoughts, hopes, and wishes are powerful. Guard your thoughts well, for by them you reach the pinnacle of success or failure.

"God does not threaten us. His promises are ever true. God is a loving Father. He gave His only Son as a ransom for us. For God so loved the world, that he gave his only begotten Son, that whosoever believeth in Him should not perish, but have ever-lasting life."

The pastor raised his arms in benediction. The strains of the organ filled the small church with ethereal chords. Nell stood straight and thumbed through the hymnal until she found the selection to close the services:

"Just as I am thou wilt receive,

Wilt welcome, pardon, cleanse, relieve, because thy promise I believe, O lamb of God, I come! I come!

As Nell left the church, she felt happier than she had in years. Indeed, she felt as pure as the lilies on the altar.

Part II
Marla
1942

Chapter 9

Marla's Family

May afternoons were always uneventful in the parsonage. A row of elms tempered the lingering winds that whispered round the house.

The Reverend Henry Hanson had delivered his sermon at eleven o'clock as he had on every Sunday for the past thirty odd years. Now, he rested in his special chair on the porch.

In one hand, he held his beloved Bible, in the other a fly swatter, It was not that the month of May produced an invasion of winged insects; he had to seem occupied. Sometimes, he interrupted his Bible reading and fly-swatting by taking a nap, which he refused to admit he indulged in. On occasion, he conversed with Ellie, his wife, or his daughter, Marla.

Marla was no longer a child. The fun-loving little girl had become almost a woman. He missed their usual afternoon game of checkers, but now

Marla was no longer interested in competitive games with her aging father. He nodded automatically in response to her "Hi, Papa," as she dashed past him into the living room.

Marla, how upset he had been when Billie had insisted upon that strange name. The Reverend Hanson had chosen a biblical name for his youngest child, but Ellie would have none of it. This child would not be named Ruth, Mary, Rebecca, or Martha. Ellie had won the round. As strange as the name had once seemed to Henry, no other would have better suited this elusive child of his. From the very first, she had tugged at his heart.

As Henry mused about the child who had gone past him like a whirlwind, a vision of his three other children occupied him. Martin, the eldest, had a degree in engineering and was living in Milwaukee.

His two older daughters, Ruth and Anna, had married fine upright citizens and were raising their children to respect God.

Often, in Henry's reflections to Ellie, his concern for Marla overshadowed his favorite topic, next Sunday's sermon.

"I can't understand Marla, Mama," he would say. "Every young person should have some kind of a goal, something to work for."

Ellie would quickly pick up a stitch in her knitting, and her comment would always be the same, "As the young twig is bent, so shall it grow."

"I guess you're right, Mama."

With his thoughts on his youngest child, Henry would then drift into his usual Sunday afternoon nap, his Bible held loosely in his lap with one finger marking his place.

Ellie had watched Marla during the entire service. Oh, she had bowed her head and closed her eyes during prayer and she had risen with the congregation at hymn time, but her actions had seemed hypnotically controlled.

Ellie did not condemn her child for this; many times she had behaved in the same way. It wasn't that Henry's sermons were dull or that he wasn't a good preacher. It was just that his words were always tried first on Ellie and Marla. Only after their approval were they delivered to his flock. The frequent repetition of Henry's sermons had blurred the impression.

Ellie feared God. Although she was certain that Henry had been called to the ministry by God Himself, she sometimes assumed that his interpretation of the Good Book was not entirely accurate.

There was an amazing contrast in the background of Ellie and Henry Hanson. Henry's father had been a minister as his father had been before him. Ellie was the daughter of Jake Zumstein. Old Jake, as Mr. Zumstein was called more often than not, was known for laxity both as a family man and as a working man. As a father, he was lenient to the point of allowing his daughters to attend the theater, dances, and card parties. They were also permitted to use lipstick, power, and the curling iron.

The artificial and sinful lures which the Zumstein daughters used to attract the young men was a cause for social discussions among the not-so-worldly women in Preacher Hanson's church, especially those who had their eyes on the preacher's son.

The calming effect in the Zumstein ménage was Hannah, Ellie's mother. Hannah was short and stocky. A woman so gentle that many could not imagine how she had ever been attracted by the rough, cursing Jake.

In the large family of nine children, the religious training was meager. It consisted of a once or twice a year attendance at an Easter or Christmas celebration held in the one-room schoolhouse, some eight miles distant.

No explanation was needed as to why the Zumsteins did not attend Preacher Hanson's church. It was a known fact that Old Jake had an occasional bout with the bottle, notably on Saturday nights.

Then, with nine children, there was the problem of feeding and clothing them on the lean wages of a farmhand. The girls took turns wearing the dress-up dresses their Aunt Hattie sent them, but the older they became, the more reluctant they were to wear their cousins' hand-me-downs.

It was extremely embarrassing, Ellie often recalled, to sit in Sunday school, clinging to worn hankies and pretending there was a penny tied in the corner. "It was worse sitting in church without money than sitting there without shoes," Ellie had once told Henry more than once.

Ellie glanced now at her husband, slouched in the chair, and mentally measured the breadth of his shoulders. The sweater she was knitting would be large. He used to have such broad shoulders, she thought, remembering the first time she saw him. They were building the new parsonage, and she walked by three or four times before he noticed her. Then he called for her one Saturday night. Her father was drunk and cursed in front of the preacher's son. And she had cried, certain that she would never see Henry again. But the next weekend, he was back.

Ellie could never figure out why Henry Hanson, bombarded by objections from his father, could possibly have fallen in love with her. There was one thing she had promised herself as a young girl; she would never marry a farmer. Later, she had wondered at times if a farmer would have been a better choice, but somehow, the love she felt for Henry could never have been given to anyone else.

Ellie relived a bitter experience. On her fourteenth birthday, her Aunt Hattie invited her to spend the day in the city. It was a Sunday and they planned to attend an evening service. Ellie borrowed a hat and high heels and the biggest purse her cousin Beth had.

Mesmerized in the pew, Ellie drank in every word the minister spoke, regarding it as a personal message. Blinded by tears, she worked her way with the throng to the altar and accepted Christ as her Savior. Tears of joy and submission overwhelmed her. She had given herself to Jesus.

Her heart sang. She, Ellie Zumstein, was a Christian. When she returned to her seat, she closed her eyes tight and clasped her hands. She was saved!

The collection plate was passed. Ellie dug deep into her oversized purse and deeper until she reached the lining. The quarter had disappeared among the assorted oddments. Her face flamed. The ushers, embarrassed, left without her contribution. Her tears burned even deeper when the minister pounded the rostrum and said, "How dare you sit with empty purses while the sins of the world rest on your shoulders?"

The whole world did rest on her shoulders; in fact, the whole world collapsed. Her personal heaven was destroyed in a second, destroyed by the wave of a hand and the words of a devout man of God.

The woman who had appeared in a moment of wonder became again the little girl of seven who pretended she had a penny tied in the corner of her hanky. She had walked forward and given her soul, but she did not have one thin dime for an offering.

Even during the years as a minister's wife, the memory could not be erased. In confusion, she questioned her husband.

"Dear," Henry would reply, not always patient, "that minister did not direct his statement just to you, but to the whole congregation. Unfortunately, you had lost your offering and felt guilty. The church must have money to exist."

Henry's explanation never satisfied Ellie. *Is God a cruel judge as many preachers interpret Him or is He the loving God my mother taught me to pray to?*

Ellie reviewed the number of times she had prayed, prayed until her heart ached and tears flowed. Again and again, she went over the route in her memory. Heartaches, illusions, dreams. *I prayed that Mama would live, but she died. I prayed that I would not have another child, but Marla was born.*

Her ungodly prayer. A life grew inside her, and she prayed that it would not be born. Already a grandmother, she was pregnant again. Fears were magnified; she was going through the change, and menopause babies were sometimes born deformed or mongoloid.

But the baby was born. The nurse lay the baby in Ellie's arms. It was wrapped in a pink blanket and it cried. Ellie did not want to look at the child, but tiny fingers curled over her own, and when she looked at the child, it was beautiful and perfect. Yet there was an emptiness inside, intruding on her privacy. Dr. Blakely sensed her reluctance. He put his hand over hers.

"Ellie, you were convinced your childbearing days were over, but you have a beautiful, wonderful child. You are very fortunate, when other women are growing old, you will stay young because of her."

To the same degree that Ellie felt bewildered and unhappy, Henry felt a deep pride. Ellie wanted Henry to feel as she did, somehow ashamed that they experienced so close a relationship at their age, but Henry was elated. *That old goat is actually proud of his manhood,* she thought. It was the closest time she had ever come to feeling disgust for Henry; it was also the time she realized how much she loved him and needed him.

Ellie prayed many times during those first few months of Marla's life. Silent, weak prayers, afraid that God would not answer them. When Marla got colic, Ellie was certain it was a punishment from God for her sinfulness. How could her milk provide sufficient nourishment when she had harbored such sinful thoughts when she was carrying the baby? When Marla was four months old, Ellie reluctantly put her on the bottle.

Eighteen years later, Ellie thought, *the child I did not want is the very one that has made my life worth living. Praise God for His infinite wisdom.*

Chapter 10

Marla's Music, and honoring her father

The napping Henry's ridiculous snores brought Ellie back to reality. His mouth was wide open and he looked odd. He had been a big man, but age had made him smaller. His old-fashioned glasses had slipped down his nose and the few hairs left on his head were bristly like a boar's.

Marla glanced mischievously at her mother and touched a piano key.

"Mama, watch." The strains of an exhilarated polka floated out to the porch.

"Marla, you know your father does not allow that kind of music on the Sabbath."

Noting music foreign to his ears, Henry nearly choked on his snore. He put his hand to his head and jumped straight out of his chair. By the time he was fully awake, Marla had switched to a sweet, sedate hymn that had been sung at the morning service. Ellie joined in a duet. Henry sat back in his chair, wondering what had riled him. He thumbed his way back to the scripture he had been reading.

"Mama, you should sing at church instead of Mrs. Thompson. Her voice is scratchy."

Ellie stopped humming. "Dear, a minister has to be careful not to let his family take over the duties of the congregation. I remember when your father was called here. Reverend Olson had a very talented family. His wife was an accomplished organist, and they had two lovely, talented daughters. They held the top offices in the young people's group.

"They had a son too, a friendly young man. He was head usher. They all taught Sunday school, in fact, they covered about all the needs of the church. Well, the church kept going downhill. In fact, some of the members stopped attending. They felt left out, it wasn't really their church.

"There were only a handful of people in the congregation when we came. It wasn't long until they told us their grievances. We then made it a point not to make the same mistakes."

"I didn't know that, Mama. I just thought that Rev. Olson was one of those old hell-fire preachers, like Grandpa."

Ellie was startled. "Like Grandpa?"

"Oh, I used to hear you and Papa arguing. You always told him to put more of God's love into the sermons. I remember once you told Papa that Grandpa spoke more about hell than heaven."

Ellie put her finger to her lips, cautioning Marla against speaking of her departed grandfather in such a fashion.

The conversation faded and an oppressive silence filled the house. The only sounds were the flip of the pages as Henry read his Bible and a deep sigh from Marla.

"Is something bothering you?" Ellie asked Marla.

"Mama," Marla said softly. "I've met a boy, rather I've been seeing one."

"That's nice. Does he go to our church?"

Marla hesitated. "No, but he's terribly nice. His name is Frank Henderson, he's captain of the football team. He's going to graduate, and he's dreamy."

Ellie knit frantically. This type of conversation was inevitable. She had gone through it all before, but this was Marla. Seventeen is so young, eighteen, she smiled remembering Marla's coming birthday. *At eighteen, I had already given birth to Martin and expecting Anna.*

"He asked me to go with him to the prom," Marla was saying.

Ellie patted the sweater she was knitting. "You'll have to ask Papa. Better wait till after supper though."

"You know what he'll say. It isn't fair, I can't do anything because he's a preacher. Everything fun is sin."

"Depends on what you call fun," Ellie said, smiling.

After dinner, Ellie and Henry retired to the living room. Marla stayed in the kitchen preparing an apple pie; the dessert would be the cushion for the favor she intended to ask of her father.

Marla glanced apprehensively at her mother as she served the pie. Henry patted his stomach and sat back comfortably in the big chair, reading the paper.

Marla sat down on the arm of the chair. "Papa," she announced prematurely, "the prom is Friday night."

"So," Henry answered, not raising his eyes.

"Frank Henderson asked me to go with him."

Henry sat very still, but Ellie could see his knuckles whiten as he clutched at the paper tighter.

"Can I go with him? We'll probably double date with Larry Cline and Esther."

"No!" There was no misinterpreting Henry's verbal reply. "No daughter of mine is going to make a fool of herself dancing with some young hoodlum."

Tears came to Marla's eyes. "How can you say that? You don't even know Frank."

Henry was visibly upset. "Can't you just see Mrs. Bloom get a hold of something juicy like that? I'd be the laughing stock of the town."

"Henry," Ellie intervened. "Marla is a good girl, she should be allowed to date, and it is the prom, Henry."

Henry stared into the paper but did not look at Ellie.

"If I recall, Henry, you told me yourself that you wished your father hadn't been so strict with you."

"Tommyrot!" Henry said, throwing the paper down and stomping from the room.

Marla begged, pleaded, and wept to no avail. Henry was a strict disciplinarian and strong-willed. Nothing could sway him from his convictions. He was the head of his household as well as the head of his church.

Ellie did not relish going against Henry's wishes. *He's so pig-headed,* she thought. Try as she might,

Henry's God was not always her God. She would take things into her own hands. Marla would stay overnight with Esther. Henry would be so involved with his church work that the yearly celebration would slip by unnoticed or so Ellie hoped.

Henry came home from the financial meeting later than usual. He wearily climbed the stairs to their room without speaking to Ellie. And Ellie knew she had been wrong. She had let Marla go with Frank Henderson, a boy that did not belong to Henry's church. And she had allowed Marla to attend a dance, and dancing was a sin.

Frank was holding Marla close as they danced.

"Baby," he whispered. "My folks flipped, gave me the keys to the Ford, the car's mine until I go in the Marines."

Marla's heart was beating so fast, she hardly knew what he was saying.

"Let's go for a ride around the lake," he said, dancing her to the door.

"Frank, are you crazy?" she said, but when he looked at her, she melted. He ran his fingers gently over her back, and she felt a strange excitement. When he put his lips to her throat, she trembled.

"I'll go, if you promise you'll have me back here before the party's over."

"Scout's honor," he said.

They walked quickly past the chaperones. Marla took her coat from the locker. Larry Cline looked up as they were slipping through the door.

"Heh, Henderson, don't do anything I wouldn't do," he shouted.

Marla clutched her coat tightly. It wasn't right, but she was going to go. She was going to leave the school ground against the rules of her parents and the school.

Frank and Marla had walked along the lake shore in the daylight, but tonight, he parked the car on the road that wound above it. The lake below them mirrored the silvery birches that grew along the bank. Frank took the car robe from the car and spread it on the grass, drawing Marla down beside him.

The sound of crickets and frogs seemed deafening until Frank's lips were on hers, then there was only the thumping of Frank's heart against her own. She was swimming in emotion. *This,* she thought, *is what worries Papa.* The shame of Frank feeling her nakedness. A vision of her father in the pulpit came to her and her grandfather preaching hell fire.

"Not this way. Please, Frank, not this way," she pleaded

Frank was strong, but not nearly as strong as Marla's convictions. Her moral obligations to her parents won over all his persuasions.

"Marla, it has to be now, we might not have another chance. It will be all right, I promise."

"No," she said, straightening the folds of her dress.

Frank grabbed the car robe, shook it out, and tossed it into the back seat. *It's as if he's done that a hundred times,* she thought.

Driving back to the school, Frank didn't talk to her.

He opened the car door, and she stepped out.

"Are you mad at me, Frank?"

"No," he said, still not looking at her. "You know why I couldn't, don't you?" "I guess so."

"Please don't be mad," she pleaded. "Look, I said I wasn't, forget it."

Marla did not intend to cry, but somehow tears came.

"Listen, Marla. It was my fault. Nothing happened, so you don't have to feel bad."

She looked at her dress, wrinkled and soiled. She had lost one of her garters from her girdle and the ribbon had fallen out of her hair. She had almost, but she didn't. Yet she felt as sinful as if she had sold herself.

The auditorium was almost empty when they walked through the door. Esther rushed to her.

"For God's sake, where'd you go?" She looked at Marla. "Come on, kid, we'd better get you home."

As they left, Marla heard Frank explaining to the chaperones. "Had a flat!" At that moment, Marla hated him for lying.

On the following Monday, they were both back at school for the final week before graduation. Larry Kline handed Marla a crumpled note. It was from Frank. "Meet me in front of the fountain, third period," it said.

How long can a class be? she wondered. It seemed to her that the third period would never come. Every time someone looked at her, she flushed. *What if Frank is like some of the other guys and brags about how far he got with me? Maybe he'll lie like he did about having a flat.*

She waited by the fountain. When he appeared, he looked older, taller, and more handsome than she remembered.

Frank glanced down the hallway to make sure there was no teacher around, then took her hand.

His eyes looked straight into hers and she was no longer sorry.

"About Friday night," she said. "I'm not a very nice girl, am I? Teasing and not going through with it."

"You're not the teasing kind. I just shouldn't have expected you to come across like that. I'm sorry, honest I am."

The bell rang, and Marla started to leave. "It's all right, Frank. I forgive you."

Frank clung to her hand as she pulled in the opposite direction, knowing that she would have to leave, wanting to stay near him.

"I'd better hurry. I'll be late for class."

"Think your dad will let me take you out before I go?"

Marla thought for a moment, then her eyes gleamed as she had found the answer.

"I'll be eighteen a week from Sunday. I hope he won't object anymore."

The teacher peered over her glasses at Marla as she walked quietly into the classroom. All eyes turned. "Marla Hanson, take the seat in the rear, and turn to page forty-seven for review."

"Yes, ma'am."

"And, Marla," Miss Abrams added, "stay after class. You have fifteen minutes to make up."

Marla raised her eyes to the teacher, then quickly turned the pages of her book. The words were blurred and she ached all over. The tears felt hot in her eyes, and she blinked to hold them back. *Frank,* she thought, *I love you. I love you. I love you.*

Chapter 11

Sunday morning after Graduation

The Sunday morning after graduation, Marla stayed in bed. She was shivering beneath the blankets although the sunlight flooded her bedroom. *Papa will be in the pulpit,* she thought.

He'll be singing louder than anyone else. When he says something that sounds really good, he'll look down at Mama and me. Mama will smile, but I'll just sit there. Later, Papa will ask me if I liked the sermon, and I'll say as I always do, "Papa, it was good, really good. I don't think old Mr. Russell slept a wink."

But it was a lie. Today would be like any other Sunday. Mr. Russell would sit down and keep his eyes closed during the whole sermon. Sometimes, he would wake up startled, then realize he was in church and close his eyes again.

When the services were over, Mr. Russell would be the last one to shake hands with the Reverend Hanson as he left the church, and he'd cling to the preacher's hand. "Pastor," he would say, "that was quite a sermon, yes, sir!" Marla thought of Mr. Russell's watery blue eyes, his bent back, and slow gait. "Someday, Papa will be like that," she told herself sadly.

Henry knocked lightly on Marla's bedroom door, then opened it. "Time for church, Marla."

Marla pulled the blanket up over her chest. "I'm not going, my head hurts."

The Reverend Hanson entered her room, wearing his parson's robe, the white collar high under his chin. Marla thought, *He looks so Godlike. So Godlike and fierce.* Somehow, the two adjectives did not seem to belong together.

He touched her forehead. "Shall I call Dr. Blakely?"

"No, Papa," she said. "I'll be OK."

"Sure now?" He was so concerned. He looked down at her, wishing she was a little girl again and that he could pick her up and hold her. "Wish you could hear my sermon. Mama says it's one of the best. It's the one on the prodigal son."

Marla flushed. "I'm sorry, Papa, I would like to hear it. I really would."

"Now, I know you're sick. Sure there isn't something I can get for you before the services start? Breakfast? A glass of water?"

He started to leave the room. "I'm sorry I didn't let you go to the prom, I guess I've been awfully strict with you."

"Papa," she called after him, "I did go to the prom."

Henry swallowed. "I know. I've known your mother too long for her to pull the wool over my eyes."

"Papa, say a prayer for me."

Henry felt a lump in his throat. He had forgiven her as easily as if she were the little girl again. *There is so little time,* he thought. *Soon she'll be going to college, and Mama and I will be alone. Time has a way of going so swiftly…it sneaks by, until one day you're old and stooped, and your mind has a way of looking backward. Marla is a woman now, eighteen, yet I can only see the child.*

"By the way, when are you going to bring your young man home for Mama and me to look over?"

"Soon, Papa, soon."

He patted her head again. "Happy birthday, honey."

"Thank you, Papa," she said, keeping her eyes shut to hold back the tears.

She heard the door slam as her mother and father left for church. Her head really did hurt. *I didn't lie,* she told herself, *I really am sick. I've gradu-ated. I've graduated from the tummy ache to the head-ache.* She tried to sleep, but sleep would not come. She was too busy remembering.

She was five, maybe six, and she had visited her grandfather's church. Her grandfather was louder in the pulpit than her father. He shouted and gestured with hands raising them toward heaven, pointing them downward to emphasize hell.

She sat very still between her mother and father. Grandfather was preaching about sin and the devil; she had a tummy ache and started to cry. Mama carried her out to the church lawn and she vomited in a bed of petunias. Afterward, she felt better, but she refused to go back into the church. Papa had been unhappy about it, but she stayed sick until she was back in her own bed.

She was eleven or twelve and was away at church camp, a skinny kid with knobby knees and small lumps for breasts. She wore long skirts, longer than those of the other kids. She was a preacher's daugh-ter and had to be more reserved. There was a boy there—maybe he was a preacher's kid too—and they both had the same dirty blonde hair.

Someone asked if they were brother and sister, and that was funny because he had ideas that brothers should not have, with sisters that is. They sat beneath a big tree and talked. He touched her in places little boys should not touch, and he kissed her. She did not feel different; she felt just like she always did.

When they reached the camp, she had grass stains on her dress and the stains went through her dress and thin cotton slip and to her panties. She tried to wash them out, but the stains remained. She bundled the clothes into a neat little package and hid them under her cot. She told her mother that she had lost them, but a day or two later, she found her dress, neat and clean, hanging in the closet. She wondered what her mother had done with the panties.

Later in the afternoon, Marla felt better.

"Have you thought about your major?" Henry asked, his heart set on the state university.

"I haven't made up my mind yet."

Then one day, she announced without prompting or questioning, "I'm not going to college, Papa. Frank's coming home next week and we're going to get married."

Marla saw Frank as he stepped off the train, tanned and hand-some, searching the crowd for familiar faces. She saw him in the arms of his father, mother, and younger brother. Then his mouth was on hers and her heart was thumping. *Never,* she thought, *will I refuse him again.*

Surprisingly, Henry did not rant when Marla spent all her time with Frank. Sometimes, she would come home from a date, drenched to the skin, her hair stringing down her back, and her face flushed. Marla noticed that her father looked past them, not at them. He looked weary and he had grown thin. Ellie had called Dr. Blakely, but medical examination had failed to show anything of an alarming nature. Henry was like a man who had lost a great battle, and Marla knew that the battle had been with Ellie. Ever since she could remember, when there was a serious conflict in regard to discipline, Ellie won.

A few days before Frank's furlough was over, Frank and Marla were married. Ellie wept, not knowing why, perhaps it was because the baby she had not wanted was now a woman. More probably, it was because she too felt the pain which Henry had concealed so well.

Time did not allow a formal wedding. There was no flowing white bridal gown nor was she surrounded by a maid of honor and bridesmaids. Marla wore a street-length dress of pale blue and was attended only by Esther and Larry. Though Henry beamed as he blessed his daughter's marriage, his heart was heavy.

The church arranged a reception, and members of the church attended, some whom Henry had not seen for weeks. Some pitied him, but all respected him. A shepherd of men, he was not exempt from disappointment and earthly burdens. Being a man of God did not imply that his every wish would be granted. It only meant that he suffered more keenly when life went against his principles.

Summer passed, and fall came, changing the leaves to orange and gold, then brown and drying. The days shortened and winter came. The latest news was that Frank was somewhere in the Pacific. Marla hid her concern for Frank in the pregnancy she could no longer conceal. Many of the congregation had counted the months on their fingers, and Henry was certain that Mrs. Bloom was fussing and fuming, wondering if the days would add up correctly.

Several weeks passed, and finally letters from Frank ceased to arrive. Marla was becoming more uncomfortable daily, and the dark circles beneath her eyes advertised the fact that she was not sleeping.

It was difficult to write to Frank when there was nothing to say. Sometimes, it seemed as if there had never been a Frank, never a marriage, and never a child that kicked and squirmed inside her. But each morning, she started the letter, "My darling husband," and ended it, "Love forever and always."

The Wilsons, Hanson's next-door neighbors, had received the dreaded message that their son Gary was missing in action. Marla prayed for Frank silently, while inside her fear nagged, destroying her faith in good and in God.

April arrived. It was nearly a year since Marla had graduated from high school. *A year ago, I was happy,* she thought. *I wasn't even in love. In less than a year, I have become a woman, married and carrying a child. I have a husband somewhere. I've written letters and had no answers. I can cry all night with no one to hear. My baby will be born and I will be alone. A year can be so short yet so much can happen. Larry and Esther are married. Papa is much older and Mama worries about him. And when I think of Frank fighting in some faraway jungle, I want him so much that I want to die.*

Later in the spring, a messenger brought the telegram. Henry answered the door and took the telegram. The words on the yellow paper were blanked out by his tears.

"It's Frank, Mama. Frank is dead."

Ellie rushed to his side and took the telegram from his hands. She sank into a chair.

"Frank's dead, my poor baby, my poor baby," she crooned, thinking only of Marla.

"It's my sin," Henry wept. "I didn't want Marla to marry him. God is punishing my child for my sins."

"No, Papa," Ellie soothed, "it's not anyone's fault. It's the war, this damn senseless war."

"Mama," Marla appeared in the doorway, "what's the commotion about?"

Noticing their tears, she dropped her hands to her side, the color faded from her cheeks, and she collapsed in a small heap on the rug.

Nothing could protect Marla from the pain. Henry held her close, weeping with her. Ellie wept too; hoarse sobs that made Marla gasp in wonder. It was the first time that Ellie had cried in her presence. It was her cross too.

The unborn child stretched and kicked. Marla was not disturbed. She sat through the memorial services her eyes straight ahead, walling among the flowers, her hand holding Frank's hand. Frank at the prom, Frank at the station, Frank in the marriage bed. She was lying close to him and felt his hard body. She was smiling into his dark eyes. They were laughing together, and they were crying together.

A dream? she wondered. There is no casket, only flowers. In her mind, she ripped the petals from the flowers and let them fall around her, walking barefoot over them, feeling them between her toes. She felt the coolness on the soles of her feet and tears spilled down her new dress and her garter was broken, and the ribbon lay soiled and wrinkled on the front seat of the car. Frank was shaking the car robe, and the grass was falling over her. She was shouting and she was weeping, "No, Frank, no!" but it was only in her mind. Frank was dead—dead, like the petals she had crushed into the dust—on a faraway island whose name she had never heard of until the telegram came.

A flood of misshapen faces and bodies pressed against her. Some rubbing wet cheeks against hers, some clasped her hands and she felt strength, some were tender and gentle.

Voices, some soft, some questioning. Frank's mother caressed her, but formally.

Marla walked out into the sunshine, keeping close to Henry and Ellie, though they seemed only shadows. Later in the silence of her room with darkness around her, the pain of losing Frank was more overbearing than the pains that ripped through her body.

"Frank!" she screamed and screamed in a nightmare. They were screams of a woman in the agony of childbirth, a woman unaware that she was screaming.

"Mama," she sobbed when the pain had subsided. "I feel as if I'm going to break in two."

Twelve hours later, finding natural delivery impossible, the doctors resorted to Caesarian section. Steven Blaine Henderson weighed in at six pounds, eight ounces. But Marla Henderson was a long way from either her memory of Frank or the knowledge that she had delivered a child. She did not respond to drugs or to expressions of love. Yet in God's strange way, though Marla preferred to die, she lived.

Chapter 12

Marla's baby

Summer had come again, hot and sticky. Then, before Marla was aware of it, August and September were gone and it was fall. Winter came, and for a while, time seemed to stand still.

It snowed hard and the snow clung to the trees, the rooftops, and the telephone wires.

Then as if the world had awakened from a long sleep, a warm wind stirred and melted the snow and ice. The snow slid down the roofs; the trees shook themselves free, revealing their green buds. Crocuses and tulips spread a whisper of color over the land. Almost overnight, the lawns turned green again. Marla was awakened by the sunshine that streamed through her window. She looked out at the world and everything seemed new. It was as if she had been on a long, long voyage and was home again.

Ellie had taken over most of the baby's care. She dressed him, fed him, and took him for walks. Once, during her pregnancy, Marla had jokingly asked, "Mama, how does a new mother know what to do when she has a baby?"

Ellie had smiled. "Don't worry, honey, when the baby comes, you do what comes naturally."

The sight of Marla laughing and playing with her baby brought pleasure to Henry and Ellie. They had been patient. Soon, they said, she'll get over her grief. How long they had waited.

Now, Marla awakened each morning, happier than she had been for years. She bathed the baby and fed him joyfully. She started to play the piano again and joy returned to the household.

It was on Stevie's first birthday that Marla brought a letter onto the porch to read to Henry and Ellie.

"I got a letter from Lucille," she said. "Frank's older sister. She wants me and Stevie to come to the West Coast awhile. It sounds exciting. I've got the money from Frank's insurance, so I wouldn't be sponging on them."

Ellie was stunned. "Aren't you happy here? We love the baby, and when you are ready to work, I just heard they need a girl at the new store."

Henry lay his Bible down. "Maybe Marla's right, Mama. A trip would be nice for her. We can watch the boy, and she can have a vacation."

Marla picked up Stevie and held him close, a frightened look on her face.

"No, Papa," she said, "I want to find a job there. Sooner or later, I'll have to get out on my own. I'd rather not stay here, imposing on you and Mama."

Henry dropped the subject, picked up his Bible, and started to thumb through the pages. Ellie sat looking out of the window. Of course, she couldn't expect Marla to spend her whole life at home, but it was frightening to think of her so far away, and with the baby too.

In the evening, they had a birthday party for Stevie.

Ellie had spent all day on the cake, icing it with mountains of white foamy frosting. She put a tiny blue boat in the center and a candle. It was a gala occasion, with Stevie strewing the wrappings in all directions in search of the brightly colored toys.

After the party, Ellie helped Marla pack.

"Maybe you should think it over a bit," she ventured. "Stevie, it will be hard traveling with a baby."

"Mama, I've made up my mind," Marla said impatiently. "I just have to do something on my own, just once."

Ellie held the stuffed rabbit she had made for the baby in her hands. "We'd better leave this out," she said. "He can play with it on the way. He always liked this one specially."

"Mama, it isn't that I'm ungrateful," Marla said. "I appreciate all that you and Papa have done for me. You understand, don't you? I just have to live my own life. So far it's been one big mess. Everything I do seems to hurt you more."

Ellie turned her face so that Marla could not see the tears. "Darling, you've never caused us unhappiness. I, we, only want you where we can help you if you need us. It isn't easy to raise a child alone."

Marla's own tears streamed down her cheeks.

"Explain it all to Papa," she begged. "I would rather die than hurt you again."

"Marla, that's sacrilegious to talk that way about dying. We only want you to be happy."

"I know that, Mama. I know you do." She looked at Ellie questioningly, hoping there would be no answer. "Mama, you talked Papa into letting me go out with Frank, didn't you?"

"You were eighteen, you were old enough to decide for yourself whom you wanted to date."

Marla folded her hands wearily and sat down. "No, Mama, I wasn't old enough, not really. I never even kissed a boy before I met Frank, oh, maybe once, then when Frank joined the Marines and left, I could hardly remember what he looked like. It was like a dream. I knew a boy and he went away, but when he came home on leave, I knew he was the only boy in the world for me. I had to hurry and marry him. He was going away and I was afraid I might never feel that way about anybody again. You see, Mama, how war makes you think? You're always afraid. I was afraid I would never see him again and I didn't. In a couple of days, we lived a lifetime. Do you see why I had to marry him?"

Ellie held Marla close. "I know, dear, that's the way things hap-pen sometimes. We don't really plan it, but it happens."

"But I made Papa so unhappy. He wanted me to go to college like Ruth and Anna. I couldn't, Mama."

"Baby, it's only natural for parents to want an education for their children. Marriage and children are great responsibilities. Being a minister does not make your father less vulnerable. Sometimes, *we* set our hopes too high."

"Mama, let's not talk anymore tonight. I'll get up early and we'll have breakfast together just like we always do, and then…" She never completed the sentence but picked up the baby and walked toward the stairway. Ellie watched her. Marla looked like a sad little girl with a tear-smudged face, tugging at the child as if he were a rag doll.

Ellie heard Henry drop his shoes and snap off the light. But she stayed up. There were many things on her mind. The wind whistled through the screens on the front porch and the sound of it sent a chill over her. *Might as well go to bed too,* she thought, although she knew she would not be able to sleep.

When she slipped into bed, she heard Henry snore and smiled, remembering how she and Marla had joked about it, especially on Sunday afternoons when he napped on the porch.

She also thought of the time when, if God did not choose her first, she would be alone. There would be only memories then, memories of the happiness and sorrow they had shared.

Ellie quietly tiptoed from her bed to Henry's. When she tried to move him over without awakening him, he groaned. He looked so small lying there, but she could not budge him.

"Marla, where's Marla?" he murmured, half awake. "Marla's in bed, move over, I can't sleep."

She was like a child when she couldn't sleep. She nestled against him, feeling warmth and strength. He put his hand on her breast and sighed contentedly. She kissed him softly on the lips.

"Henry, I love you," she said. He held her close, and they slept.

The morning sun was red and warm, and although it was the day Marla was to leave, there was an almost cheerful atmosphere. Marla's dog Friskie followed her from room to room, though for the past few years, he had slept most of the time, hiding under the back stairs at the approach of the creeping youngster. He had usually growled at the baby. Friskie was old and almost deaf, and the quick movements of the child startled him.

Today, the baby tugged on his fur, at his ears, but the dog merely lay in the kitchen doorway or scampered after Marla. It was as if he too knew he would be separated from his mistress.

The only sounds in the parsonage after Marla and Stevie left were the creaking of Henry's chair, the soft footsteps of the dog as it wandered from

Ellie to Henry for a pat on the head, and the sharp clinking of kettles as Ellie worked in the kitchen. The piano was seldom touched, the doors were seldom banged. The house without Marla and the child was silent.

Henry went to the post office more frequently. When no letter came from Marla, he was depressed and frustrated.

"What did I do wrong, Mama?" he asked Ellie. "I wanted so much for her, but I let her down when she needed me most. Sometimes," he said it under his breath, "I wonder if there is a God."

Ellie gasped and set the pen down with a bang. "Henry Hanson," she demanded, "how can you say such a thing? You were brought up in faith. How can you possibly even think such a thing?"

He was sorry he had said it and thoroughly wished he could take it back. Ellie followed him to the porch and picked up her knitting.

"You know, I've been thinking, perhaps Marla's marriage, her having the baby, and Frank's dying are some kind of a sign."

"How's that, Mama?" Henry glanced up quickly, knowing full well that Ellie was leading to a discussion of his last few sermons. He knew they were not up to par. He was dry, his mind was not functioning the way it used to. Words that had come easily had to be prodded. And when they came, they were stilted and awkward.

"Lately…" She searched for a way to say it without injuring his pride. "Henry," she said swiftly lest she lose the desire to say it at all, "you sound more like your father every day, money and hellfire."

"I hadn't noticed," Henry said squabbling. "The financial committee has been after me because we've fallen short on the budget to finish the church basement."

"I know that too, but you can't scare people into giving. Henry, preach more about love. Tell them." She did not know how to express herself. She went to Henry and sat on the arm of his chair, laying her hand gently on his shoulder. "Darling," she said softly, "tell them that God's love is free, that we don't have to buy God's love. Some churches make you feel that you have to have money even to go to church."

Henry closed his book with a snap and stood before Ellie. "Some people have money to burn, but they hang on to it as if it were their last dime. So we have to beg. Do you think I like standing there in the pulpit, trying to squeeze a few measly bucks out of each one so the church won't collapse?"

"Then, my dear, you have missed your calling," Ellis snapped.

Henry sat back down in his chair, painfully, as if life had somehow left him. Ellie's words could cut sharply, and the wound would be deep.

"I think you're right," he said. "God forgive me, but I think you're right." He wanted to shout, "Shut up, shut up. Do you think it's so easy to be a preacher? To hear your words fall on deaf ears, to put the Bible into words they want to hear instead of words inspired by God Himself, to preach forgiveness of sins, when they don't even feel they are sinning?"

There was a time when Henry had not intended to be a minister. He winced remembering the fall from the scaffold, the ribs digging into his lungs, the traction in the hospital, the day he was told that he would never lift another brick or trowel.

His father had come to him then and he had been forgiven for his marriage to Ellie Zumstein, his fall from the grace of God. The prodigal son returned to his father. His father arranged for the years at the seminary. There had been nothing else for him to do. Anna was a baby and times were hard. Almost before he was aware of it, he was in his own church. He never forgave himself or his father. He was a failure then. He was still a failure.

Ellie noted the look of despair on. Henry's face. Marla's leaving had upset him, and somehow she always said things at the wrong time, in the wrong way.

"Henry, I didn't mean it that way. You're a good minister. I just can't forget that I came from a poor family. We didn't feel welcome in church. It didn't matter to Pops, but it did to Mama."

Henry was visibly upset. He was as concerned for her soul as for his own, but how he wanted to forget she was a Zumstein! He wanted her to forget it too.

"Did I tell you about the time I went to that big church in Milwaukee? I sat there snug with that big pocketbook I had borrowed from Beth. Henry, I didn't have even a penny to put in that collection plate. I felt like a thief."

If Henry had heard that story once, he had heard it a hundred times, so for the hundredth time, he attempted an explanation— anything to stop her nagging. "Dear, you took that as a personal insult, perhaps he could have chosen other phrases."

"But it's true," Ellie rattled on. "The minute a person with prestige moves to town, the churches break down their doors, trying to entice them into their midst. Then, if they don't pledge or give what is expected of them, they are criticized and snubbed until they feel guilty and quit coming.

"Then a poor family comes along or a Negro family, and they're ignored. Henry, how many times have you invited Mr. Leland to our church? He's a Negro and just a janitor."

"I've asked him a number of times." Henry rose from his chair, then sat back down in it. He hated himself at the moment; it was a lie, and Ellie knew it.

"Pops used to say," Ellie stormed, "that if a farmer sowed five bushels of wheat and harvested twenty-five, that did not mean he should tithe on the twenty-five but only on the twenty, which was the increase. Why do some churches insist on a straight ten percent?"

Henry lowered his chin until it nearly touched his chest, pulling his glasses down on his nose. He peered at Ellie over the frames. "I preach to give so you'll prosper. Honor the Lord with thy first fruits, so shall thy barns be filled with plenty. Give and it shall be given unto you in increased measure."

Ellie always weakened when Henry quoted scriptures.

"I seem to be in a bad mood," she said. "I've been upset and I'm taking it out on you."

"I don't agree with you, dear," he said with a twinkle in his eye. "I'm taking out my weaknesses on you."

Henry looked at the clock. "Coming to bed, Mama?" he said, the twinkle still there.

Later, they were getting ready for bed. Ellie seemed to be in a pensive mood and stood by the window, looking out into the night.

"Henry," she said, "I'm worried over our church."

"That's nothing new. I've had a few worries myself."

"Not only our church, Henry, all churches. I think we're losing sight of God in our concern for material things. I know I'm just as much a hypocrite as the next one, but I'd like to open our doors and call out so the whole world can hear. 'We have a Savior and it doesn't matter what color you are or how much money you have or how full of sin you feel you are.'"

Henry sighed. "It's all right to preach love for all from the pulpit, but trying to implement that concept is another matter. If I preached the way I wanted to, we'd be looking for another parish, and at my age, I'm just not up to it."

Chapter 13

Marla leaving home

Marla Henderson sat rigid in the bus seat, her parents far behind her now. She was alone with the sleeping child who lay heavy against her. She wished she were back home. She closed her eyes and rested her head against the seat cushion. Bits of conversation, occasional laughter, the cry of a child, or the giggle of a teenager kept her from sleeping, so she adjusted her position and watched the scenery.

Slowly, they emerged from tree-covered hills to miles and miles of rocky ledges, jutting in a grotesque design into the skies. Green valleys nestled between hills, with winding streams. Then came miles and miles of shimmering grain fields, miles and miles between towns, with here and there a lonely house. It was miles to a bus stop, and there was no time to eat when you reached it. A quick sandwich, a cup of coffee, a hurried visit to the restroom, and the trip was resumed.

Darkness for miles and miles and miles. *Stop, go, stop. Oh, God,* Marla thought, *if only I could sleep. I wonder what day it is,* her thoughts ran on. *Stevie is so damp. Wet, I suppose, perspiring too. It's so hot.*

I've got to make a home for him now. I can't depend on Mama anymore. I can't impose on Lucille either. I've never worked before. How will I ever find a job?

Darkness again, the moon big and round, and the stars scattered in a haphazard pattern. *I feel sort of sick, must be sage brush land.* Fences, the lights of a big city. Another stop. Forty minutes this time.

She ordered a cup of coffee, some milk for Stevie, and a cheese sandwich to eat on the bus.

Stevie's wet again. Oh, God, why can't he? Why didn't I wait until he was trained? How can I work and take care of him too? Wonder what Mama and Papa are doing. It's Friday I think. Papa's at the financial meeting, or do they meet just once a month? It seems as if I've been riding for months instead of a couple days.

Ellie had suggested she fly or take a train. But she had insisted on a bus because she wanted time to think, time to get used to being alone. Well, she really wasn't alone.

She had the baby, didn't she? Why did she still feel alone, as if the baby were nothing? *Mama was right of course.*

Mama was always right.

Finally, she slept. When she awoke, they were at another bus stop. Stevie was crying, and he had vomited on her skirt. *I could just wring your little neck,* she thought. *Why do I think those awful things?*

She kissed the baby and murmured,

"Mama loves you, sweetheart!"

I'm so tired, she thought as she rubbed her soiled shirt with a handkerchief. *I shouldn't blame him.* She shook his bottle and discovered that the milk had curdled. She took her paper sack of dirty diapers, the bottle, and tucked the baby under one arm. A colored soldier assisted her off the bus, and she thanked him. She thought of Frank. It was hard to imagine that Negros were dying in the war too.

Inside the restroom, she wet a paper towel and wiped Stevie's face and then her own. She threw the bag of soiled diapers into the wastebasket, hoping no one saw her. There was not enough time for a meal, so she rinsed out the baby's bottle and had it filled with fresh milk and bought a bag of popcorn for herself.

The contour of the land had changed now. They were driving into low hobnail mounds, but she could see the purple-misted mountains in the distance. Going through the mountains, she found it was hard to swallow and her ears hurt. They went through a snow-covered passage where the highway was as narrow as a ribbon, flanked by gullies that looked bottomless.

Four more hours, she thought, *four more hours and I'll be there. I wonder what Lucille is like. Wonder if she looks like Frank.*

Marla dug deep into the side pocket of her purse for Lucille's phone number and address, then called a taxi. She was in a strange city, alone with a crying child. It was a big city, foreign looking, with tall buildings and wide streets. The people were hurrying in and out of the depot, and she felt a welcome relief when she climbed into the cab. There was a dark sky overhead, rain splashed against the windshield, and the driver was talkative.

The lawn was green and the shrubbery grew close to the windows. Marla could see the curtain pulled back from the front window as the cab halted. She knew that they were watching her, wondering what she was like too. The driver carried her luggage to the door and waited while she rummaged through her purse for change.

There was a lump in her throat, and she struggled with the baby, trying to make him quit crying.

"You should have phoned, we could have met you," Lucille Maddox said.

Marla was pleased that she had dark eyes like Frank's. The baby stopped crying when Lucille crooned to him.

"Coffee? Have you had your breakfast? I'll run the bath water," Frank's sister said all in one breath.

"A bath!" Marla ran her fingers through her dusty hair and looked at her clothes in dismay. "A bath. Oh, how I need a bath."

"The towels are on the rack by the basin," Lucille called from the kitchen, "and there's soap in a dish by the tub."

Marla reached for Stevie. "I'd better wash him first. He's been fussy."

"You take your bath, honey. I'll stick him in the kitchen sink, washed all my kids there when they were babies. Coffee's on."

Marla searched her luggage for her hairbrush, found it, and started toward the bathroom. Lucille called up to her, "Better lock the door, the kids forget to knock."

Marla could hear Lucille humming, and Stevie had stopped crying.

The water was hot, and she sank into it gratefully.

There was a bottle of green shampoo on the drain. She reached for it, poured the cold liquid onto her scalp, and massaged her hair briskly, then scrubbed her body until the flesh was pink, soaped the cloth, and rubbed some more.

She's nice, Marla thought, thinking of Lucille. *It's almost like being home. Only I can't stay, I can't stay.* Suddenly, she was not happy anymore. She would never be really happy again, not really. Her tears splashed into the murky water.

The weeks she had planned to stay with Lucile stretched into months. She took a job as a drill press operator in a war plant, and when she got her first check, she moved into an apartment with another war widow. Florence worked the day shift; Marla worked at night. It was a solution to the problem of Stevie. Florence was childless and seemed happy to have the baby around. The arrangement was convenient for both of them. Florence was there in the evenings, Marla was home all day, a tired, cross Marla, desperate for proper sleep, fearing to indulge in it too long. The hours at the plant were long, but the pay was good, and there was not enough time left to think about Frank.

In time, Marla became accustomed to the moods of the big city. Seattle, with its dismal, smoggy, dreary mornings, with its fall rains, wind-blown torrents, a slow pattering, downpours falling straight from the sky, or a steady drizzle that lasted for days or weeks.

Seattle the beautiful! Sunny, brisk, sparkling green Seattle— peppermint green, chartreuse green, olive green, fir green, and the startling blue green of the sound.

The kaleidoscope: the blue sky, the purple-violet-tinged sky, the red sky, the orange and yellow sky.

Seattle the industrial—fishermen, lumberjacks, salesmen, farmers, shipyard workers, aircraft. The working woman, white uniformed for the hospital or doctor's office, for the waitress and bakery, in slacks for the factory, in coveralls for the defense plant, in street clothes for the home or office.

Seattle, home, the alarm clock, the time clock. There was no variation in the daily routine.

Then suddenly, the war was over and the world was jubilant. Bands played, newsmen joked, mothers wept for joy, servicemen were reunited with loved ones. The heart of the nation began to beat again.

While the people celebrated the victory, Marla's world crumbled. Something had died within her a long time ago. Her Frank would never come home. The defense plant had closed down. And Stevie had the measles.

For weeks following the war's end, Marla's life halted. There were no alarms to listen for, no time clock to punch, no reason at all to get out of bed in the morning. Pure boredom urged her to look for another job.

Marla stepped off the bus in front of the cafe. She glanced at her reflection in the window glass before entering.

She had lightened her hair earlier in the week, and she was a new Marla. The lighter color was flattering. It made her eyes look bluer, and she looked younger. *Too young,* she thought.

A navy-blue suit made her figure look boyish, slimming her hips that had expanded gently with her pregnancy. The lapel pin, a cluster of gold leaves subtly enhanced her costume. She looked, she decided, like any of the career girls who were in search of positions.

Marla straightened the seams of her hose after taking a quick look around to make sure no one was watching.

She entered the cafe and chose a table in a corner.

"Any luck?" the waitress asked, as she brought coffee and a thin slice of cake.

Marla broke off a small piece of cake and put it in her mouth. After she had swallowed, she said, "Nope, it's the same old story, lack of experience. There are a few openings for waitresses, but I couldn't even balance a cup of coffee on a saucer."

Her feet hurt, and she slipped out of her shoes, glancing around to see if anyone noticed. The line at the employment office was long, just like standing in line for a pair of nylons during the war, except that at the end of the line, there had been a pair of nylons.

She finished eating the cake and sipped the coffee slowly, watching the customers.

"Boy, that sure looks good!" the tall, thin man at the counter told the waitress, as he turned on the swivel stool and faced the window.

"Sure does, Mr. Denson. It sure is an improvement. That old building was downright disgraceful. You sure fixed it up."

Marla heard her name mentioned, and the man glanced at her. She flushed and blotted her lips with her napkin.

She was about ready to leave. As she rose from her chair, Mark Denson addressed her, "Winnie told me you're looking for work. I may just have something. I'm opening my office right across the street, I could use a receptionist, someone to answer the phone, meet customers, and type a little."

"I can type, I had two years in high school. I'm not very good, but I would practice."

Mark Denson took a deep breath, appraising her at a glance. "You might just fit the bill." He looked at his watch. "I've got to beat it now. Maybe you can drop by my office in the morning. By the way, I'm in insurance, you name it, I sell it."

Chapter **14**

Marla gets a job at an Insurance Agency

ay by day, week by week, month by month, Marla lived the insurance business. To her nine-to-five hours, she added two hours at night school, mastering bookkeeping, sales fundamentals, and advanced typing. She hungered for the knowledge that was necessary for her success and the success of Mr. Denson's business.

At the office, she felt the security of the clients, the friendship of Mr. Denson and his wife. It was at night when she was alone, and Stevie had been tucked into his bed that the past flitted before her eyes: the little church, her father in the pulpit, the tear-stained eyes of her mother, Stevie as a baby, and then as a little boy. There were memories of Frank too: Frank the high school hero, Frank at the prom, the wedding, and the flowers of the memorial services.

Then ironically, Frank's body was returned to Wisconsin for reburial. Marla told herself that she would not go home now; she would not subject herself to the torture of another burial service. When her mother sent her the flag from the ceremony, Marla folded it neatly and put it in a cellophane bag with the rest of Frank's mementos. She could not sleep that night.

Stevie lay asleep, his hair damp and clinging. She brushed the hair from his forehead and kissed him softly on the cheek.

"I've neglected you so, darling," she murmured. "Now, you're getting so big. You never knew your daddy and you've never really had a mother's love, not love like Mama gave me. Mama always tucked me in and said my prayers with me. I never had time to read to you or say your prayers with you. Only when Florence was in California. Remember, honey, how lonely it was. I was home with you for a whole week." Marla nudged the sleeping child. "Did you say your prayers, honey?"

The child still slept. She recited the prayer: "Now I lay me down to sleep,

Angels guard my little nest; Glad and well may I wake, I ask it all for Jesus's sake.

"You mustn't forget to say your prayers," she whispered. The child moaned and turned away from her.

Unable to awaken her child, Marla rummaged through the drawer that held Frank's memories. "I feel so awful. I feel just like I did that night I called Dr. Morrie, that was when I still worked at the defense plant, the week Florence was in California."

She found the bunch of Frank's letters and the little gold football. Letting the football dangle from its chain, she placed it around her neck and started to read the letters. When she had read all the letters, she gathered them in a neat stack and tied them again with the chain. She was crying. *A ritual,* she thought, *weeping for the dead. The same old depression. I can feel it, like a thread connecting me with the living. Someday, that thread's going to break.*

The almost tragic night came to her mind again, the night Stevie had said, "Mommy, I don't think you love Daddy anymore or you'd love me."

Those weren't the exact words, but she couldn't remember the phrasing; it was lost.

She was saying the same words to Stevie as she said that night, "Of course, Mommy loves you. Mommy works so hard and is so tired. Mommy's sorry she's so crabby sometimes. You forgive Mommy, don't you?"

Oh God! I feel just like I did that night.

That night, she had the strangest feeling. Stevie was already asleep, but she had awakened him wanting him for company. She read him a story, and he had gone back to sleep before she had finished it. Then a vision of Frank came to her; he was holding out his hand to her and wanted her to go with him.

Then he vanished; just as she was going with him, he went away.

Frank wants me with him, she thought, surveying the means at hand. The brown bottle of sleeping capsules, the blade from the razor she shaved her legs with. She emptied the bottle of aspirin on the table; there must have been a hundred tablets. It took her a long time to pick them up again, putting the pills back into the bottle one by one. Shaking, she slammed the mirrored door of the medicine chest close and strolled to the window. The cord dangled from the draperies long and white and strong. The draperies flew back as she yanked the cord. Across the city, she could see a bridge—water dark and cold and deep. She imagined herself drifting in the foam.

"Happy birthday, honey." A camera flash of memory. "Papa," she wept. "I wouldn't hurt Papa."

I'm going crazy, she thought, reaching for the phone as she riffled through the yellow pages.

Physicians, running her fingers down a row of names, she found a psychiatrist and dialed.

Dr. Isador Morrie answered the phone.

"I need help," she whispered into the phone. "I've got to see a doctor."

"Is it possible to wait until morning?"

"No!" she screamed. "I've got to see a doctor now. I'm afraid I may kill myself. I want to die. I don't want to live!"

Marla lowered herself into a chair; she was shaking, and she was cold. *I shouldn't have called him. I know I wouldn't kill myself, no matter what. It's just a feeling, not really me.* She tried to pray, but the simplest prayer refused to come.

She folded her hands and said, "Please, God, help me in Jesus's name."

It was nearly two-thirty in the morning when the short bespectacled Dr. Morrie knocked on her apartment door. She opened the door for him and let him inside. He talked quietly, and she answered his questions anxiously, trying to sort out the information. There were some things she could not reveal. She told him about losing her husband overseas, about her father and mother, bits and pieces about her child. She answered so many questions that finally she could not remember what she had told him and what she had kept back.

The doctor recognized a state of hysteria and administered a sedative. She gave a little gasp when the needle went in and the doc-tor's face faded. She heard a voice in the distance. *Papa,* she thought. *Papa is with me.*

She was sleepy, but she heard her voice still answering questions. The voice seemed to come to her from a tall mountain,

"Ten o'clock." She heard herself saying, "Ten o'clock."

She had a very pleasant dream. She was in the little white church, sitting next to Ellie, and she was wearing a white Swiss organdy dress and new white sandals. Old Mr. Russell was wide awake, his watery blue eyes blinking with emotion. Her father was young again, and his voice was strong as he delivered his favorite sermon, "The Prodigal Son."

The next morning, she called Lucille and asked her to watch Stevie. At ten minutes to ten, she was in the doctor's office. There was another patient in the reception room, and Marla wondered why she was there. *I shouldn't have called him last night,* she thought.

"How are you today?" the doctor asked Marla.

"I'm fine, thank you." She wondered what he was thinking. "Did you sleep well last night?"

"Sleep? I didn't even hear the alarm clock this morning."

"Tell me, Marla, you were very upset last night, you mentioned a feeling, a sensation. How often does this occur?"

"I really can't say. Sometimes, it's sort of vague. Last night, it was awful."

"Can you describe it in words?"

"No, it's just a feeling. I wouldn't know how to put it into words. I just felt strange. It has something to do with Frank. No, I can't describe it."

"You said last night that your father is a minister. Did you like being a minister's child?"

"I never thought about liking it. I was a preacher's kid. Sometimes I couldn't do things the others did, but I don't think I resented it. Papa was very strict about some things, but I didn't get upset about it. I took it for granted that I should be different."

"Did you ever do anything against the will of your father?"

Marla looked at him questioningly. "No, I thought I'd like to, but I never did. In my mind I did, but not really."

I won't tell him about the prom, she thought. *I won't.*

"How do you mean that, in your mind?"

"Oh, I used to imagine that I was doing certain things, like dancing or dating with somebody I knew Papa would disapprove of."

"That gave you a certain satisfaction?"

"I imagined it did. I was only a child. It was sort of daydreaming. Doesn't everyone daydream sometimes?"

"Yes, Marla. I believe we all try and escape into fantasy at times. When you phoned me last night, you said you were afraid... afraid that you would commit suicide. Was that the truth? Were you serious?"

"I don't think I would have done it. I pray to God that I wouldn't have, but I don't know. I didn't feel like myself. I thought of Stevie and how he'd be better off. I've always sorta neglected him. When he was a baby, Mama took care of him. I had that crazy feeling, and I wanted to get out of it."

There was a knock at the door and a nurse came in. "Mrs. Hodges is waiting, Doctor," she said.

Dr. Morrie opened his desk drawer and took out a prescription pad. "Have this filled. Take four a day. And make an appointment for next week."

Marla rose from the chair. A few moments before, it had seemed a nice friendly chat. Now the doctor was very professional. Marla rushed to the door and fumbled for the knob. Dr. Morrie opened the door for her and said, "Marla, call me. I think those tablets may help. When are you going back to work?"

"The girl that shares my apartment will be back this weekend. She went to California for her father's funeral. Monday, I'll go back Monday."

"It may take a little time, Marla, but I'm sure I can help you." "Thank you," Marla said, walking quickly out into the street.

Dr. Morrie was certain that he recognized Marla Henderson's malady. He had several patients who had lost loved ones during the war. Normally, there would be a few months of despondency, then the person would miraculously adjust without therapy. There were some who would not, or could not, accept life with its daily cares and burdens. For some strange reason, they remained in a world of their own for months, even years.

Marla puzzled him. She was young, seemingly intelligent, and certainly attractive to the opposite sex, but she seemed to be almost happy clinging to a memory. He would have to dig deeper.

He had concluded that being the youngest child of aging parents, Marla had never been given responsibilities as a child, that as a minister's daughter she had been protected from the harsh realities of life. Though her father seemed to have been strict, her mother had been overprotective, perhaps to hide her own guilt.

On the third session, the doctor probed her past in search of the Marla of the present. She seemed unusually jubilant when she entered his office. He questioned her casually about her work, her child, and her health, trying a new approach.

"Marla, how do you spend your evenings?"

"I work nights at the defense plant. I have weekends off." "How do you spend your nights off?"

"Sometimes I visit with Lucille. She's my husband's, Frank's sister."

The doctor leaned back in the chair, his hands folded. "Do you ever go to a movie or have a date?"

"Yes, I go to a movie once in a while with Florence, when we can get Lucille to watch Stevie."

The doctor cleared his throat. "Do you ever go out with men?"

Marla fumbled with her keys. "I don't know many men. I work with some of them, but most of them are married."

"Have you been out with any man since your husband was killed?"

"A few, most of them don't want a date. They're looking for something else."

"Do you mean sex?"

"Yes." She flushed.

"Doesn't that seem to be a normal part of dating?" "To some people probably."

"How do you feel about sex? You've been married. The subject shouldn't be embarrassing."

"I really don't know. Outside of marriage, going all the way is a sin. It's against the Bible."

"You feel strongly about that?"

"It's been pounded into me as long as I can remember."

"Marla," he said in a fatherly way, "Frank is dead. Nothing can ever bring him back. You have a child. This child needs male companionship, you need male companionship. You should be thinking of remarrying. Sex is a normal part of life."

She looked at him strangely. "I don't want to think of marriage again, not yet."

"Do you have something against marriage?"

"For me, yes. I don't ever want to feel again the way I did when Frank..."

"The war is over. There is little chance that you would lose your next husband."

"I didn't mean that, Doctor. Once, before I was married, I was out with Frank and I loved him so much that I almost let him. I didn't, but I felt guilty anyway. Afterward, I wished I had gone all the way because it couldn't have made much difference. I felt just as bad as if I had let him. When we did get married, everybody, including Mama and Papa, thought I had to get married. I didn't have to, but the baby came early because I was all mixed up on account of the memorial services. I couldn't prove that I didn't. To this day, I know Mama and Papa think I had to."

"That was a long time ago, Marla. Time goes by and people forgive and forget. And you know the truth."

"I know I do, but it still bothers me."

"Life is for living, Marla, you have to take the bad with the good. You cannot build a wall around yourself and shut the world out. You have a long life ahead of you. It would be unnatural to spend it alone without love, without sex."

That was her last visit to Dr. Morrie. Now several years later, she was feeling the same way again; she'd heard of a relapse, but she wouldn't let it happen.

She tried to read but put the book down after reading a few pages. Maybe she should try again to wake Stevie; he'd be better than nothing. The child was determined to stay asleep. She picked up the phone book, searching for Dr. Morrie's number. It was no longer in the phone book. *I'm glad,* she thought, *I've got to get over this by myself. What good would it do? He'd just give me more pills and lecture me about my physical needs. I just need someone to talk to.* Aloud, she said, "Marla Henderson, you've got to think about Stevie."

She had made her decision, and in time, the memory of Frank grew dimmer and dimmer. Sometimes, she wondered if it had really happened at all.

Dr. Morrie was right, in some things, she thought. *I need companionship, male companionship.* She reviewed the men she had dated through the years. Lonely men in search of lonely women. Platonic friendships and affairs. And just last week, she had met John Hilton; he had been different, she didn't feel so guilty anymore, but dreams about her parents were getting more frequent. Nearly every night, she dreamed about her mother or father. *Maybe Mama's sick or Papa, they're getting so old. Maybe it's a warning. I should go home.*

One morning soon afterward, Marla reached for the phone and dialed long distance. Steve's voice came over the wires.

"Mother?" he said, surprised. "Mother, are you all right?"

"I'm fine, darling," she said. "I'm going to take a vacation, go back to Wisconsin."

"What brought all this on?"

"Oh, Mama and Papa are getting old. I think I should spend some time with them. Steve, I've decided. I'm going home!"

"Sounds like a great idea." He sounded unmoved and cold, almost as if she were not his mother. "Give them my regards, Mother," he added.

She held the receiver to her ear until she heard him hang up. *My baby,* she thought, *Mama loves you.*

She emptied the drawers from her dresser and began to pack. She started to hum. *Mustn't think,* she told herself, *or I'll change my mind. I'll have to call the airport and make a reservation. I should call Lucille, and I'll send a wire to Mama.*

"I'm going home!" she sang. "I'm going home."

Chapter 15

Going home for a visit and meeting David Wright
Marla 1962

*T*he morning Marla was to leave for Wisconsin, the airport was fogged in. As Marla walked to the window to view the grounded planes, she felt uneasy. She hated delays. It had taken such a long time to decide to go home, now she was anxious, and the weather had to delay her.

There will be snow at home, she thought, *unless there's a late Indian summer. The sun will still be warm and Papa will be on the porch. Mama will go out and wrap a shawl around his shoulders. Wonder if he still swats at those flies. Mama never says anything in her letters, but she's getting shaky. I can see that. Her letters have been getting shorter all the time.*

I hope Mama hasn't changed anything. The living room had a sort of gold-colored wallpaper. I can't remember the design, but it was old-fashioned even then. But oh, how I would love to see it just the way it was. I'd like to walk up to the door and kiss Papa on the head. He'll be so happy. Oh, what's the use? Things change. It won't be that way, never can be the same again.

She walked away from the window and sat down on a hard bench. A few minutes later, she went to the information booth and asked, "How soon will the plane leave for Chicago?

"The fog should lift in an hour or so." They had said that three hours ago.

Marla reached for the paperback she had tucked into her purse and opened it. The letters blurred. Her glasses!

She had almost forgotten she wore them; going home had made her forget little things like that. She put her glasses on and scanned a few pages. The book was dull; she stuffed it back into her purse.

She sat as rigid as a statue. A man sat down next to her. She smelled the scent of his shaving lotion and glanced at him from the corner of her eye. He was dressed neatly in a dark suit, a businessman. He seemed impatient too. She smiled at him.

"This waiting is awful, isn't it?"

He smiled back. "Sure is, guess they'll be able to take off in about forty minutes. Going east?"

"Wisconsin, I'll have to catch a bus the rest of the way."

"Great, we'll be on the same flight. I'm on my way home, Pennsylvania. I have to stop in Chicago on business though."

There seemed to be nothing more to talk about, so Marla drew out the book again. This time, she kept her eyes glued to it, although she did not really know what she was reading.

It was a best-selling novel, but it seemed to be extremely verbose,

"All passengers on Flight 507 will now board at gate 3," roared the loudspeaker.

"That's us." Marla arose excitedly, gathering up her purse and coat. She sensed that the man followed her closely up the ramp of the plane.

Marla took a seat near a window. The man smiled as he passed, changed his mind, and came to her seat.

"Do you mind if I sit here?"

She picked up her purse from the adjoining seat. "No, you can sit here if you like."

He was very attractive, she now noticed, middle-aged, and his hair was graying. He had the bluest eyes.

The light in front of the plane flashed the order: Fasten Your Seat Belts! No Smoking Please. Marla fumbled with her seat belt and tried to adjust the chair to an upright position as instructed by the stewardess. The seat wouldn't budge. Marla blushed.

"Let me see if I can get it." He bent over her, pushed the button, and the seat flipped up.

"I just wasn't pushing hard enough," she explained.

The plane was off the runway. Marla stiffened. It was the first time she had been in a plane. *Hope I don't get airsick,* she mused. They had been in the air only a few minutes. The street scenes diminished in size. They were already flying above the clouds. The clouds looked like giant cotton balls floating on a big blue lake. The river below was like a narrow ribbon. Then there were only the clouds below them.

"Your home in Wisconsin?" the man asked.

"Wisconsin?" For a moment, Wisconsin seemed so far away, almost a place she had never heard of. "Yes," she said, "my parents. I've lived in Seattle for almost twenty years. Time sure flies. My son is in college. I'm a widow."

"Vacation or do you plan to stay?"

Another question, one she had not thought of having to answer, not yet anyway. "My parents are getting old. I just wanted to see them before it's too late,"

"Oh, by the way, I'm David Wright. I've just been home too. Visited my brother. The first time in nine or ten years."

He looked at her and their eyes met. He understood how she must feel; he had had to go back to the old place too. Everything had been strange. The house had been remodeled. Even the orchard looked different. The old Larson house had been torn down and another house had been built, a modern one.

The only thing that hadn't changed was the pear tree. It had grown larger, but the bees were still in it.

"Everything had changed. I almost wish I hadn't gone back. Oh, I shouldn't say that. I don't want to spoil your visit."

Marla sighed. "You won't spoil anything. I want it to look the same, but I know it won't. Nothing stays the same."

The stewardess appeared with lunch and coffee. "Cream and sugar?" she asked, as she served them.

"Black," they both said.

They finished lunch, and Marla glanced at her watch.

They had already been in the air for three hours. "These planes, time sure flies."

"It does," he said, "if there is someone to talk to. Time can go mighty slowly sometimes."

She concentrated, thinking, remembering.

"I know. Some days can seem like a week. I forgot to introduce myself. I'm Marla Henderson."

"Marla," he repeated.

For several minutes, they were silent. Marla closed her eyes, pretending to sleep. The pilot made an announcement, giving the altitude, flight speed, and location. Marla opened her eyes.

"Whew! Thirty-two thousand feet! We wouldn't have much chance if anything went wrong, would we?"

David Wright laughed. "Everything seems to be under control, Marla," he said. "I've been thinking I only have to spend a few hours in Chicago. Don't have to be back at work until Monday. Maybe you'd let me call on you at your parents' home. You could show me the sights, and we could get to know each other. You know," he put his hand on her arm, "this may sound crazy, but I think I've been looking for someone like you for a long time."

She took a slip of paper from her purse, wrote down the address, and handed it to him. "I would like that," she said.

The elms that lined the street had grown until they nearly hid the house from sight. As Marla stepped from the cab, it seemed to her that she was in a strange neighborhood. *Must have painted the house,* she thought. *It looks different, so small.*

She knocked lightly on the door and waited for someone to answer. *No snow yet,* she reflected. *I expected to find it at least two feet deep, but it's only October.*

She heard a familiar voice and a shuffling of feet. "Come in, the door's open."

She entered the house almost fearfully. Her mother looked so much older; her hair was almost white.

"Mama," Marla wept, "I'm home!"

Ellie held her close, tears rolling down her wrinkled cheeks. "Oh, Papa will be so happy to see you! How is little Stevie? Marla, you are a poor correspondent. Why didn't you write more often?"

"I don't know, Mama. Mama, you should see little Stevie now. He's over six feet tall. He's going to college."

"Yes," Ellie said reminiscently, "it's been a long, long time. Come see Papa."

Henry Hanson sat in his faded old armchair. His body was crouched down in the padded chair so that he almost seemed a part of it. He clutched his Bible tight in a shaking hand. The few hairs remaining on his head stood straight up. His mouth was thin and his cheeks hollowed. He was snoring.

Marla signaled Ellie to watch Henry. Then she lifted the lid of the piano and, with one finger, struck a note.

Henry grunted and opened his eyes in surprise. "Marla!" he said hoarsely.

Marla flung her arms around him, kissing his head and lips. "Papa," she wept. "Papa, how are you?"

His chin quivered as he lifted his hands to caress her face. As Marla's hot tears fell on his hands, his own tears came. He ran his fingers gently over her face, feeling the bone structure beneath the skin.

"Mama," Marla whispered. "Papa's blind! He can't see me."

"He's been that way for about two years," Ellie said. "He's failing fast. Oh, Marla, how he has grieved for you!"

"I know, Mama. I was awfully wrong. Oh, God, Mama, I hurt Papa so."

Ellie held her child to her breast. She held her for a long time until the tears stopped.

Later, after the dinner dishes were washed, Marla and Ellie joined Henry in the parlor. Ellie picked up her knitting, and Marla played a few of the old-time hymns on the piano. When she stopped playing, she went to her father and sat on the arm of his chair.

"Marla," Ellie said, "you haven't changed much. The years seem to have been kind to you."

"I tried to keep busy, Mama. Sometimes, it was awfully lonesome, I couldn't forget Frank."

"Oh, how Papa and I worried about you! You were so far away. I even thought of going to see you, but I couldn't leave Papa."

"I should have come sooner. I just wasn't ready, I guess, Mama," she said, her voice vibrant. "Mama, I met the nicest man on the plane. He's going to come here to see me. Is that all right, Mama? To have him come here?"

Ellie glanced up at Marla's face. Marla's eyes were shining as they had shone when she had told her about Frank.

"That's nice, honey," Ellie said. "Isn't that nice, Papa? Marla has met a nice man."

"How's that, Mama?" Henry bent his body forward to catch her words.

"Marla has met a nice man," she repeated in Henry's ear.

The shawl dropped to the floor as Henry Hanson arose.

He held his Bible in both hands and the pages flipped open to one of his favorite passages. In his senile mind, he was in the little white church again. He scanned the faces of his congregation until his eyes fell upon Ellie and Marla. They were sitting quiet and receptive in the front pew. Henry Hanson launched his favorite sermon by recitation:

"And he arose, and came to his father. But when he was yet a great way off, his father saw him and had compassion, and ran and fell on his neck and kissed him.

"And the son said to him. 'Father, I have sinned against Heaven, and in thy Spirit I am no more worthy to be called thy son.'

"But the father said to his servants, 'Bring forth the best robe, and put it on him; and put a ring on his hand, and shoes on his feet: And bring hither the fatted calf, and kill it; and let us eat, and be merry: For this son was dead, and is alive again; he was lost, and is found.'"

Part III
Wrights

Chapter 16
The Wright family
1079

Silas Wright swayed back and forth in the tall rocker, the smoke from his pipe billowing into the night air. The crickets chirred and the frogs croaked. Now and then, he could hear the splash of an old bullfrog as it leaped into the irrigation ditch.

The hoot of the loon, the chirpings and croaking blended with the strains of the organ and Becky Wright's melodious humming so that it was one song—a sad song with a haunting, unidentifiable melody.

The rocker creaked louder as the organ tones diminished and the night sounds faded. Only Silas's thoughts were active as he viewed the day's happenings as if through another's eyes.

It was nearly dusk when he drove the buckboard to the barn. His wife, Becky, was tending the new peas that seemed to shoot up in the garden overnight. She dropped the hoe and ran to meet him.

"How many trees did you plant today?" she asked excitedly, as she helped unbuckle the belly-band from the harness.

He looked toward the orchard. "Everyone, except this little squirt of a pear tree. It must have gotten mixed up with the apples by accident."

She reached for his hand, her eyes twinkling as she spoke in the drawling Southern accent she affected when she was teasing him. "An' it didn't seem fitten to put one lil' ole pear tree mid all them apples, so you fetched it to the house, where you could watch it grow."

Silas was not in the mood for comedy, so she quickly changed the subject.

"Silas," she said, "every day you're coming home later. You're working too hard. Come, supper's ready."

Her concern for him warmed his heart, and he hugged her as they walked toward their rough-hewn home.

With her hair in a knot, the gold dimmed by strands of gray, and premature wrinkles around her eyes, the pock marks were more conspicuous. Becky looked older than her thirty-seven years.

A wooden tub was propped on two chairs in the center of the kitchen floor. Heavy denim work clothes were soaking in it.

"Who's working too hard?" Silas wanted to know. "Did Tad and August fetch you the water?" He glanced around the crude hut. "Hunting rabbits again?"

Becky set the huge iron kettle on the table, then went to the door. "Tadeus, August," she called, "time to eat."

She was afraid that Silas would reprimand them for not fetching the water, so now she approached him, speaking quickly before her sons entered. "Leave 'em be, they're too young to worry and fret like us grown-ups. I'm feared that when they grow up, there'll be another war. Hear me, Silas? Let 'em be."

The evening meal was eaten in haste. Later, Silas watched Becky scrub the clothes, then he took her red hands in his and dried them gently on a towel.

"I'll wring them for you," he said.

Becky completed the kitchen chores as Tadeus and August sat by the fire playing checkers. Silas took his pipe and retired to the veranda to his favorite rocker. Many things were on his mind as he wondered if it was fair to leave Becky and his sons alone so much of the time. Each spring, he left for the upper valley and returned with a load of young apple trees. The next months were spent planting, pruning, and cultivating. At night-time, he was so exhausted, he would go to bed with the setting of the sun. Sometimes, he did not move until the cock's crow awakened him the next morning. A deep hunger gnawed at his soul, but he could not define it.

The organ music had subsided, and Silas peered through the door. His sons had gone up to bed, but Becky had a basket of mending before her; it would be some time before she could relax.

Weary from the day's labor, he was about to retire when he remembered the little pear tree still aboard the wagon. In lantern light, he went to the barn for the shovel. The moon was high and full. He dug a hole deep and wide, put the tree in the hole, then stamped the soil around it solidly. He pumped water and poured it generously over the roots of the newly planted tree. The pear tree planted, he went back to the pump and washed his hands.

A strange feeling came over him; all this had happened before.

As the cool water washed the soil from his hands, it looked like blood. The moonlight was playing tricks on his mind. Pictures from the past flashed chronologically through his mind. He had been living a lie; he wasn't Silas Wright at all. He was a doctor. Dr. Samuel Worth, a deserter from the war, the Civil War.

Chapter 17
The War

Cannons thundered, jarring the cots where the wounded lay in rows on worn blankets or moldy hay. Some clung hopelessly to life, entrails lying outside the broken bodies until sure fingers had sewed the gaping holes.

Dr. Worth wandered from cot to cot.

"How are you, son?" he asked, as he paused momentarily to answer to a pathetic plea. As he approached a dying soldier, he reached for his Bible and solemnly read the Twenty-Third Psalm: "The Lord is my Shepherd, I shall not want. Yea, though I walk through the valley of the shadow of death, I shall fear no evil."

When the last breath was drawn, he drew the blanket gently over the face. The lad was scarcely seventeen.

A cannon blasted and millions of star-flecked particles of molten lead rained down on the weather-beaten canvas. The flash illuminated the grisly scene. A shout, a sob, a threshing of wounded men as they tried desperately to extinguish the flames.

"Lord!" the doctor said, his voice barely audible, "the supplies!" But he did not flinch nor his hands tremble. Big hands held the surgical knife delicately and surely, cutting the jagged wound, picking out lead fragments with the deftness of a watchmaker. Blood spilled onto the soldier's thin chest; blood covered the cold steel of the scalpel. Time was the important element. Quickly, effortlessly, the gaping wound was sutured.

The surgery completed, Dr. Worth dried the perspiration from his brow, then washed the blood from his hands. The water was cold, and he sloshed it over his arms and face. It was up to God now; he had done his best, but as he walked out into the night, the slim chance of the soldier recovering haunted him. Without sterile bandages and medications, it was a toss-up whether this boy would live or die.

The sky was dark blue, nearly black. Stars were twinkling sparks that flashed white, gold, then white again.

In the tents across the way, voices blended as they sang, "Home Sweet Home." Someone was whistling the tune. He went back into the tent and fell onto a cot and slept.

"Doc," someone cried and he sprang to his feet. To the men, it seemed as if Doc never slept at all.

Still, there was something to cling to—hope! The Northern troops were gaining ground, but losing souls.

Throughout the night, men cursed and, like children, called for Mother or God.

Dr. Worth neither cursed nor wept. He labored until fever and chills dulled his brain, and his mind was confused. Mary Beth became entangled in his torments. Mary Beth, soft and warm and tender, a son, wonder if he resembles me.

Mother, letters, Mary Beth, the locket. He clutched the locket with his wife's picture, tightly in his hand for fear of losing it. Finally, the days were as dark as the nights.

"I'm so cold, for God's sake, give me some blankets," he cried as the chills of malaria raked over his body.

Then, miraculously, commissary lines were restored: food, fresh supplies of quinine, and sterile bandages. With the new supplies came another doctor.

From the moment Dr. Ford walked into the infirmary, cursing the filth and hopeless condition of the men, Dr. Worth lost reality. *My men, my responsibility,* he reflected in conscious moments, but his mind was no longer orderly.

"Blood, stop the blood!" he shouted as he ran from the tent.

Cannon spray burst around him, tearing his clothing to shreds, but he kept running. Running away from blood and death. A fugitive traveling at night, resting beneath bridges in the day. Hiding in tall grass, in bullet-riddled or abandoned homes, he did not know where he was going or why; he knew he was hunted, and instinct told him to keep out of sight and head toward the North.

It was morning, the grass heavy with dew. A strong wind arose, laying the grass flat against the ground. The sun veiled by clouds failed to warm the man who lay inert beside the brush-covered trail. The uniform was tattered and grimy. Dr. Worth reeked of filth and disease. Thomas Moser climbed from the wagon and kicked at the body sharply with the toe of his boot.

"My god, a Yankee, a damned Yankee," he said, kneeling beside the soldier. The odor and sight of the man nauseated him, but he took his water jug from the wagon and wet his handkerchief, cleaning the saliva from the matted beard. He tried to force water between the lips, but Samuel Worth was too weak to drink. The soldier was close to death. Thomas Moser lifted him aboard the wagon and covered him with empty grain sacks. After being certain that he was not seen giving help to the enemy, he cracked the whip at the team and headed toward home.

The Confederates had passed through the town only a few weeks earlier, so Thomas waited until nightfall before he carried the soldier into the cellar. He can't live, Thomas thought, but the angel of death did not deliver Samuel Worth from his pain. After days of remittent fevers and chills, Samuel's mind did not function as a man. Like a whimpering child, he seemed content only when the gentle hands of Thomas's daughter Becky caressed his brow. He seemed aware of a fragrance lingering near him, soft hands touching him, and a sweet voice crooning to him as a mother soothes her troubled child. Throughout the sweltering days and cold nights, Becky Moser stayed by his side.

The war raged on. The South had lost many battles, and the morale of the Confederacy was thin. Harboring an enemy was dangerous and Thomas thought of turning the sick man in, but he saw new life in his daughter.

Becky had found someone to care for, someone to nurse. Ever since she had the smallpox, she had avoided people, especially men, conscious of her disfigurement. Now she was smiling again. Thomas could hear her now, playing the organ and singing a happy song.

Samuel heard the swish of her skirts as Becky came lightly down the steps. She stood outside his door for a moment before she entered. He had come to regard her as an angel; the rustling of her skirts was as sweet to him as the sound of angels' wings.

"They're gone now," she said breathlessly. "You can come up for a spell of air."

The fragrance of spring was in the air. The sun flooded over her until he could see only the golden strands of her hair. She held her hand self-consciously to her face, but his eyes were searching for hers, overlooking the scars.

For she was beautiful. He had been much too ill to regard this creature as a woman. But now, looking at her, his heart responded to what his eyes beheld. She was barely a woman, yet hardly a child. He ached for the touch of her.

There were no guilty feelings about his desires for her. He did not know his name, where he had been born, or that he was married and the father of a child. War does cruel and terrifying things to man; to this man, it had closed the door to the personage of Dr. Samuel Worth.

Becky frequently questioned him. "Do you remember your mother or father? Did you love her, the girl in the locket?"

Her persistence irritated and angered him.

"Why," he shouted, "are you hammering at me? I do not know! I don't even remember my name. Oh, God! Can't you see? I don't remember."

"I only want to help. You were wearing a Yankee uniform." She held out the gold locket, made him hold it in his hand.

"She's very pretty," he said. But he did not recognize the face.

Nothing could open the hidden passages of his mind. *I must have a name,* he thought, and from out of nowhere, he picked the name Silas Wright. A name with his own initials, though he did not realize that.

Early in 1865, scores of Southerners were flocking to the West; some fleeing the war, some in search of gold; Silas and his wife Becky to start a new life.

Now years later, Silas was reliving his life. The past, as if lurking in his mind, was waiting for an exact moment to release its message and destroy a man's heart and soul. Jagged hits of memories fitted together, precisely and accurately. "I am Samuel Worth, Dr. Samuel Worth."

He had washed the soil from his hands in cool water.

In the moonlight, the water had looked like blood. Pictures filmed through his mind. He remembered Mary Beth, feature for feature, the girl in the locket. His wife.

"A doctor's wife!" she had exclaimed when he received his diploma from medical school.

His own young voice mocked him, for he remembered his reply. "There will be times when I'm delivering some child, so anxious to enter our world that he refuses to wait until dawn. That's when you'll wish I was an ordinary dirt farmer."

It was uncanny how vivid the past was now.

He had a wife, a son, and a mother somewhere.

It was all so clear. A dream existence, then a war. A Civil War. The South determined to break away from the Union. Early in the conflict, he had volunteered, his marriage less than a year old. He had fathered a child, a son he had never seen.

The smoke from Silas's pipe floated into the air, and Silas sat in the creaky rocker long into the night. Page after page, he re-read the past.

"Silas," Becky's hand touched his shoulder. "It is late. Tomorrow will come soon."

He turned his head quickly, trying to recapture the present. He knew the truth and would try every effort to conceal it.

"I've been wondering if I planted too early," he said quickly, tilting his head, trying to make everything about himself appear normal. "It's still pretty wet."

"Come to bed," Becky said her voice fearful, for she had felt something strange about him. *It has happened,* she thought, following him into the house, then walked slowly up the stairway to their room.

"I'll see if Tadeus and August have enough covers," she said, stopping by the room of her sons. *They are so young and innocent,* she thought as she spread another comforter over them. *The man I have chosen to father them is someone I don't know. I don't know him at all.*

Somewhere he has another life, a life that we cannot share. She went to the room she shared with Silas and blew the candle out, undressing in the darkness as if her husband was a stranger and she feared to bare her nakedness before him.

Silas pretended to sleep when she came to bed. *How can I hurt her? She has been my life.* His mind was restless, and he could not sleep with such a distance between them. He kissed her gently on the temples, the throat, and her lips.

But the lips he kissed were not Becky's, for now he could remember Mary Beth.

How often during the years the truth had been so close to the surface. With professional deftness, he had delivered his sons. As he held each child and heard its first cry, severing the cord, agony had been there.

Then there was the time Eric Larson had his leg crushed by a rolling log. There had been the possibility that Eric would lose that leg; neighbors had said that he had met the crisis as well as any trained doctor. The truth had surfaced many times; each time, he had closed the door, driving the past deeper into his subconscious being.

If only the past could lie buried in the grave where I laid it, he wept. Convinced that Becky was asleep, Silas crept from his bed and recorded the planting of the tree in the family Bible. Surely, he thought, his sins would follow him in this life, in the next, and the next. He had planted his own tree of life, unearthing memories that could never be buried again. Precious Mary Beth would forever live in his mind.

Chapter 18
The Worth Family
1871

M ary Beth Worth coiled her long
brown hair, wrapping it neatly
around her head and fastening it

with bone pins. She slipped into a long dark shirt and delicately adjusted the ruffles of her long-sleeved blouse. Everything must be neat for she faced no easy task. She was now twenty-six years old and had decided that life was a mixture of happiness and sorrow; she had been dealt an even amount of both. Eight of those years had passed since she received the message from Mr. Lincoln. Her Samuel was missing in action and presumed lost.

Just one year she had spent as Samuel's wife. Now her son Robert was already in grammar school. She lived but a short distance from Samuel's mother, and though she had not always felt Amanda Worth a friend, it was important to her to share her future plans with her now.

As she approached the huge white-columned house which had been in the Worth family for generations, she was flushed and weary. To compose herself, she examined the garden, touching the satin-petaled roses, bending to inhale their fragrance.

The stone walk was neatly swept, the yard perfectly groomed. She had never been close to Amanda Worth, and today she felt the distance between them even more keenly.

Mary Beth tapped lightly on the door, then entered.

"Mother Worth," she called. The parlor, like the yard, was immaculate, everything neatly dusted. The marble fireplace had been scrubbed so that it glowed. Rows of books were neatly arranged on the library shelves.

The chair by the fireplace still held an impression. Amanda could not be far away. On the reading table next to the chair was the family Bible. Mary Beth reached for it and she ran her fingers over the raised gold lettering on the cover. "Alexander Harrington Worth." She had never met Mr. Worth, but she had heard that he was a good man, reserved and gentle. Amanda was the strong-willed member of the family, Mary Beth thought.

She was about to replace the Bible when a letter tumbled from its pages to the rug. Mary Beth examined it, not intending to pry, but because she recognized Samuel's writing. His hands had touched this paper; his hand had held the pen. Hypnotically, her eyes read the words he had written:

"Dear Mother: I miss you so. Please, Mother, do not be grieved for saying I love and miss my wife and child more. Do look after her for me; she is just a child.

"I need not tell you war is hell. There is not much chance for survival. Our supplies and food have been destroyed. I am the only doctor for several hundred wounded, not to mention those beyond my care.

"My hours are so long that my brain becomes fogged. Someday I fear it may snap. Should this occur, my concern is for Mary Beth.

"You are strong, Mother, I know that. I pray I may have inherited some of that strength, but it seems that I also possess my father's weakness.

"I will see this war to the finish if God grants me that, but should I become a supreme sacrifice for my country, guard my precious wife and child.

"Forgive me for whining, Mother. I do love you dearly. God bless and keep you daily in His care."

A lump came into Mary Beth's throat. It was almost as if Samuel had spoken the words. She folded the letter carefully and was about to replace it when she looked into the face of the tiny white-haired woman.

"Mother Worth," she stammered, "I did not mean to pry."

"It was Samuel's last letter to me," Amanda said with pride. She took the letter from Mary Beth and placed it in a hand-carved letter container on her desk. "Sit down, dear. I'll fix some tea. I made some cakes for Robert, he usually stops by."

"Mother," Mary Beth said gently, without malice, "you're spoiling your grandchild."

"Nonsense! Don't deny me the rights of a doting grandmother."

"Don't worry. Robert thinks you are very special."

Mary Beth was reluctant to confide in Amanda. She respected her, even had a reserved affection for her, but also feared her.

Mary Beth dropped a sugar cube into her tea and stirred nervously.

"I've had something on my mind, almost since I got the news of Samuel," she began.

Amanda held the saucer firmly, lifted the cup to her lips, and met Mary Beth's eyes squarely as she replaced the cup in the saucer.

"You have been restless, my dear," she said. "You live too much in the past. Memories are to be cherished, but they must not control you."

"I know that," Mary Beth sighed. "I must do something with my life. They need doctors. The war has taken many skilled men. Women do not have the calling men do, but surely there must be a place for me."

"And why not?" Amanda reached for one of the little cakes, broke it into pieces, and ate it daintily. "You have a loving heart and natural sympathy."

"Then you don't object?"

"Mind you, it will not be easy. A profession so dominated by men, it will be difficult to find a university which will approve, a nurse, yes, but a doctor…it hardly seems possible."

Mary Beth sipped her tea. She had found her goal, and already there were obstacles.

"Furthermore," Amanda continued, "as soon as you have made definite arrangements, Robert can come here to stay. It will save you costs."

"Are you certain that I wouldn't be taking advantage of you? Robert is such an active child. He can be very noisy."

"Robert is an active child, my dear. He will give this house life again." Amanda sat back in her chair, remembering the laughter and joy a young boy brings. "There will be mud tracks on my rug and fingerprints on my walls," she glanced at the neat array of books, "and books out of place. But it will be as if Samuel lived again."

"About the furnishings," Mary Beth said, "I'll just leave the cottage as it is. I must put it up for sale."

Amanda seemed to be listening to Mary Beth's chatter, but she was drifting back through the years. *I could have had another child, perhaps a daughter like Mary Beth or a son to take Samuel's place. But Samuel's birth weakened me.* She knew that was not the real reason she had denied Alexander the right to her bed. She had been very young then. Her nineteen-inch waist had become twenty-four inches. And the child tired her.

I was beautiful then, Amanda thought. *All the young men noticed me. Alexander was jealous, but Alexander was weak.*

He accepted things as they were said, then he had the breakdown.

I had to care for him, he was like a helpless child. Then he died, and I had Samuel to myself. I had this house and Alexander's money. Before I knew it, the years slipped by and I was old and alone.

"Every time I walk through the door, I see his chair and his desk," Mary Beth was saying, "I know he'll never sit there again. If I become a doctor, my career will be my life."

Amanda nodded, brought back from dreams to reality.

"Is this really what you are seeking?" she asked. How sad, she thought, that a young lovely woman, who should mother more children—and more important, care for Robert—should decide to follow a profession which would require all the strength of her being and deny her the joy of being a woman.

The joy of being a woman, Amanda Worth had denied herself the joy of being a woman. She poured more tea, and they drank it in silence, each engrossed in her own thoughts.

Mary Beth had matured, Amanda decided, but the lesson was Amanda's: service to others is God's antidote for pain.

Mary Beth's decision was like a tonic for Amanda. Now she would not be alone.

It was late afternoon when Mary Beth crossed the small wooded grove between the Worth's estate and her small cottage.

A light wind riffled the grass and caressed her face. Flushed with the exercise, she felt gay and stepped lightly, swinging her arms at the branches in her way. The leaves felt moist and cool, the sun was warm, and she felt alive.

But when she stepped inside the cottage, her gaiety subsided and a fierce loneliness assailed her. Here lay her past. She felt Samuel's presence everywhere. She lifted her skirts and held tight to the railing as she climbed the stairs to the attic where Samuel's precious letters were stored.

One by one, she read them, then gathered them into a neat bundle. She felt faint as she descended the stairway, but she must. Page by page, she fed the letters to the flames. The fire crackled as it consumed them. Not one trace of Samuel's love remained, only ashes.

Mary Beth wept, disturbed because she had wanted to destroy the ties that had bound her, that were claiming her mind and soul. But how could she destroy the memories?

She picked up Samuel's pen and wrote:

I marched up to the attic
Where your letters lay in a heap,
I said if I burn all your letters
Tonight I'll be able to sleep.

So I took your love letters
And I tossed them into the fire.
I watched the flames as they sputtered

Devouring those words of desire.

But then something happened.
I sat down and I wept, for
I had said goodbye to an old love
Whose letters I'd faithfully kept.

Oh, yes, I burned all your letters But sleep still
isn't in view.
Letters are things but mem'ries within
Are constantly turning to you.

Her tears flowed uncontrollably until she felt
limp.

It was too late, she would never hold his letters again. With the fire dying, a chill crept into the
room. Mary Beth stood tense. A rising wind rattled the window shutters and shook the tired leaves
from the trees. Mary Beth's heart pounded as if it
would never stop.

Amanda Worth felt an inner purity after giving
her blessing to Mary Beth's plan. Samuel had been
her only child, and many times, she had felt a hos-
tile gnawing of jealousy.

Mary Beth had robbed her of her son's love.

It is time for Robert, she thought, glancing at the clock on the mantle. She drew aside the heavy window coverings and watched the small figure come up the walk. He was whistling. How like Samuel he is. She opened the door and drew him into the house.

"Sammy," she cried, "you're home!"

Robert slipped from her embrace and regarded her quizzically. "Grandma, it's me! Robert Samuel Worth," he said the name slowly to make certain there would be no confusion as to his identity.

"Of course." Amanda studied him. "For a moment I thought… it is as if Samuel were here."

Robert spied the cakes. With one in each hand, he raced out the door and across the windswept lawn toward home.

The years ahead were long and tedious for Mary Beth. Being a woman was not an asset to a medical student. The skills of surgery were denied her due to her inferior status; men were more deft with scalpel and nurture.

It seemed the nearest Mary Beth would ever come to her goal in the medical profession would be as a midwife. At least, she had suffered the pangs of childbirth. Not one of the men could claim that.

She stood on the cobblestone street, admiring the hand-painted shingle as though the shingle rattled in the wind, drawing attention to her services. Several months passed and she could count her cases on the fingers of one hand. A woman did not inspire the confidence that a man did. She had invaded a man's world, and the results were disheartening.

When it seemed to Mary Beth that God's hand was against her, a letter arrived from a distant relative in the West.

A midwife was greatly needed in the town.

Months later, she received a reply to her credentials. If she was capable of delivering a child and caring for typhoid and smallpox cases, she would be more than welcome. Here was her calling. Across the miles, she was needed; "in demand," the letter had said.

It's strange, she thought. *Thousands of miles away, there is a need for me. How fate intervenes in the lives of people. Sometimes it seems as if one's entire lifetime is plotted before birth.*

Mary Beth was elated, but her joy was short-lived. Amanda Worth became ill. Mary Beth did not reveal her intention to journey to the new frontier. She would not leave Amanda now.

"Dear, do what you have to do," Amanda said. Frail and thin, she raised herself from her bed. "I've had a full life, yours is still ahead. Robert has been my joy and you have been like a daughter."

"You know about my plans to leave and travel West?"

"There is not much you can hide from my old eyes. I saw your face when you read the letter."

"But how would you manage? No, Mother Worth, I won't go."

"Go, my dear. Go for Samuel, and yes, go for me."

Mary Beth fluffed Amanda's pillow and replaced it.

"I wouldn't dream of leaving you now," she said. "I will go when you are well."

Amanda leaned forward, then fell back, gasping.

"Don't try to speak, Mother. Try to sleep now."

Mary Beth knelt to kiss the wrinkled brow, but Amanda was already sleeping, safe in God's care. She must have seen a glimpse of heaven because there was a smile on her lips.

Chapter 19

Son's going West

Soon after Amanda Worth's funeral, Mary Beth and her son Robert left for the West. The settlement along the Powder River, she finally reached, contained six or seven crudely built cabins, a cluster of tents and shacks. Rocky ledges seemed to emerge straight from the river as far as she could.

Straggly pine and cottonwood grew close to the water, drawing up its moisture into their base. Mary Beth felt dizzy and put her hand to her forehead. *I've traveled all the way across the land for this,* she thought. *I brought my child to this!*

She remembered Amanda's last words. "Go," she had said, "for Samuel and for me." In comparison with the sacrifice Samuel had made for his country, she decided, this was small indeed.

Mary Beth looked into the faces of rugged men, men unshaven and unkempt. But beyond their crudeness, she sensed other qualities: kindness, gentleness, and respect. She stepped lightly from the wagon. She was home.

Robert had already joined the throng of gaping youngsters. She panicked when he waved to her from a strange contraption that looked as if it would fall at any moment.

"Robert!" she shouted, but the only reply was the laughter of the men who noted her concern.

The men welcomed her; she was the doc they needed. The women retired to the background. Their hair was arranged in severe knots or loosely braided, and they were dressed in cheap calico prints. In her black silk dress and high-buttoned shoes, her hair arranged in an elaborate twist, Mary Beth wasn't a threat to them.

A miner's wife was not chosen for style or beauty. It took a peculiar breed of woman to bear the hardships, to struggle with the elements, to love a rough and rugged man.

It took a deeper love than most women could ever know, to sleep with the smell of sweat, tobacco, and whiskey. It took a help-mate with strong hands, a will of iron, the tenderness of a child, and a strong supple body, capable of performing many chores.

After that first day, Mary Beth concealed her feminine charms. She affected a no-nonsense hairdo and wore several petticoats beneath her full-skirted gingham gowns. Before she was settled in her new home, her chores had begun; nervously, she prepared for her first delivery.

Jane Wilson clung to the hand of her young husband and her knuckles were white. The pain knifed along her back and stabbed at her belly until she wanted to scream. The next one was worse, but she would not scream. She would clench her fists, and she would shut her mouth tight, but she would not scream.

"It isn't so bad, honey," she told Jeb as he squeezed her hand. "It hurts, but—" Perspiration ran down her face, and a white line formed around her mouth. She hid her face against Jeb's chest.

"Doc's here, Janie," he said. "Ye better have a boy, hear me?"

She smiled up at him as she grasped the sides of the bed. "Don't worry none, it'll be here soon." She put her hand to her mouth, biting into the flesh.

"It's bad, ain't it?" Jeb buried his face in her hair. "God, honey, I wish I hadn't brung you way out here. We should have stayed in Gulf Creek. Yer Ma could have been with you. It would have helped, wouldn't it?"

"Don't go far, Jeb, I don't want you to be far," Jane whispered.

Mary Beth motioned him to leave when another pain came. There was a flush of water and Jane looked frightened.

"It's coming," she said. "The baby's ready."

"It will still be a little time yet," Mary Beth said gently. She took Jane Wilson's hands in hers. "Your baby will be born in a little while. There will be a lot of pain, but when it's over, you won't remember it. The joy of holding your baby will be so great that you'll forget the pain."

Jane Wilson moaned, "I won't holler, but oh, God, it's terrible."

"You're going to have to help me, Janie. Think of something nice, so your muscles won't be so tight, and when you feel like pushing, push real hard."

Another sharp pain came. Jane dug her fingernails into the side of the bed and pushed.

"Be gad," said Jeb grinning, "you're a dern good doctor, jest what me and the missus ordered."

After that first delivery, life had its rewards, but Mary Beth could not deny that she lacked the one thing a woman always needs: love. She accepted loneliness as a penalty paid for attaining her goal.

He returned the hat to his head, after pushing his hair back from his forehead, and swung back into the saddle.

"Ma'am," he said, "them miners sure think a heap of you."

Mary Beth smiled, "I like working with them too."

"Would you like some coffee? Jake's got some boiling."

"That would be nice," she said, as she followed him to the chuck wagon.

The coffee was strong and hot, and it burned Mary Beth's throat. Rod Laughlin laughed at the expression on her face. "It'll kill or cure anything that ails ya."

For the first time since Samuel's death, the sound of a man's laughter stirred her. When Rod Laughlin asked if he could call on her, she readily accepted.

Mary Beth put the copper-clad tub on the stove to heat the water. She took her bath and brushed her hair until it shined. Omitting several petticoats, she dressed in a waist-slimming silk suit, then tucked a lilac-scented sachet into her bodice, and patiently waited for Rod Laughlin.

The years since Sara had died had been lonely for Rod. Now his sorrow had been softened by time and Mary Beth.

His arms ached for the soft warm flesh of a woman. The thought of another in Sara's place had once seemed repugnant to him. Now he longed to take Mary Beth in his arms.

Rod Laughlin had spent all day in the saddle and he was weary. Without stopping to change his dust-laden clothes, he flung his Sunday go-to-meeting suit into the wagon and harnessed the team, driving them hard until dust churned in clouds.

He strode confidently into the lone hotel, tossed a silver coin on the counter, and waited for his turn at the tub. After bathing, he donned the proper suit. He courted Mary Beth for nearly four months. Tonight, he would ask for her hand. He grinned happily as he fingered the wedding ring of hand-carved gold.

Mary Beth was not prepared for such an ardent courtship. She was a woman, but her first responsibility was to the miners, their womenfolk, and the children she brought into the world. Perhaps she loved him, but marriage? *How can I be a wife,* she thought, *and to bring my small black bag from cabin to tent? I would only be part of a wife.*

The visits from Rod Laughlin became less frequent. Suddenly, he did not come at all.

The nights were long, and she yearned for Rod Laughlin, but like Samuel, Rod had become a memory.

There was gray in her hair now and her hands were thin, but they were the only hands to soothe a sick child or comfort a mother in childbirth. She rode the mare less often, so the miners were surprised to see her one Sunday riding into the thicket. It was late when she returned, and she was feverish. Overwork and worry, she told herself, forgetting the small brown tick she had removed from her thigh. A week later, she was in a coma. Deadly spotted fever.

Mary Beth never awakened. A small white cross was placed above the mound on the hillside, where Mary Beth Worth was laid in eternal sleep.

Each spring at lambing time, grass covers the mound, and the hills are dotted with sheep as they are herded back into the meadows. Somehow, the sunset looks its reddest from that protected knoll, separated by only a thin mountain range from the resting place of her beloved Samuel.

Chapter 20

Tad and David Wright
1925

The passenger train clanged and rattled as it sped westward. In the dining car, Tad Wright sat eating lunch with his small son, David. The boy ate heartily, but the man had not touched his meal.

"Anything wrong, sir?" a porter questioned.
"Everything is fine. Just fine."

"But, sir, you've hardly touched your lunch."
"Everything is fine. Thank you."

"How about you, sonny?" the porter asked the tousled youngster.

"I want some more ice cream," the child said, firmly scraping the dish.

"Porter! More ice cream, please, for the young man."

The porter appeared with a small dish of vanilla ice cream and placed it before the child. The boy devoured it eagerly. Tad appeared to be in deep thought.

"Daddy," a small hand nudged him, "you look so funny. Are you thinking about Mama?"

Tad looked into the child's eyes. "Yes, son." His thoughts were still miles away.

"Will Mama come back?"

The question stunned him. How could he explain death? "No, Davie, she won't come back."

"Is that why I have to stay with Uncle Matthew and Aunt Susan?"

"Yes."

"Why?"

"Because you will start school soon."

"I don't want to go to school."

Tad took the child on his lap and held him close. "Everybody goes to school. I'll be working, and you'll stay with Uncle Matt."

The child looked up at his father's face, a frightened look in his eyes. "I'm going to stay with you!"

Tad pressed his lips to the tousled head, "Nope, I'm afraid not. But I'll come to see you at least once a month."

"How many is once a month?" Davie held up one finger. "That many?"

"That many."

Davie snuggled closer to his father. "Daddy, I don't want to. I don't want you to be dead too. What is dead?"

Tad could not evade his son's question. How could he answer? He had feared death. Could he ever explain it to his child?

"See that tree?" Tad asked, pointing to a flowering wild cherry. "It has flowers now. Last winter it was bare, it had no leaves or flowers. In a way, dying is like that. It's a sort of sleeping."

"Does Mama have flowers?"

Tad caught his breath. "No. Mama was sick, very sick. She went to sleep and God took her to heaven."

"If I go to sleep, will God take me to Mama?"

"You ask too many questions, son. Someday, God will take you to heaven, but not for a long time."

"I want to go to heaven right now!" Davie closed his eyes and laid his head on Tad's shoulders. "I can't go to sleep, Daddy, it's too bumpy."

"Just keep your eyes closed, you'll be asleep before you know it." "Can Mama see me from heaven?"

A tear from Tad's eye fell on the upturned cheek of the boy. Davie brushed it away roughly with his shirtsleeve.

"If Mama is in heaven, why do you cry?"

"I miss her. It's lonely without her."

Content with the answer, Davie snuggled down in the seat, put his head in Tad's lap, and yawned.

Tad studied the child's features, running his fingers through the blonde hair. *How much he is like Renee,* he thought, *yet his nose is like mine, his hair coloring is like mine, and he has blue eyes like me.*

Tad closed his eyes, conjuring a picture of Renee. *That's it! Davie has Renee's smile, kinda crooked. He has a chin like her and his eyes crinkle in the corners the way hers did when she laughed. Renee with her dark French eyes.* As he started to doze, he was back in France.

France 1918, he piloted the 140 horse-powered Voisin toward the railway station. A few minutes later, he was over the target. Trains sat on the tracks, puffing smoke, ready to pull out. The plane in front of him executed a semicircle, then flew straight to the point. The Germans were expecting them.

Aircraft flew at them from all directions. Tad could see the black cross on the fuselage and helm.

A Fokker was just off his left wing, then he was spinning, whirling through the sky in a dogfight. A wing wobbled, the motor sputtered and died. Hanging in midair, fighting to stabilize, losing altitude, falling. A wing ripped off, shaving the treetops, crash. The belly hit the ground, then skidded. Climbing out of the cockpit and running, looking back, red and orange flames shooting from the fuselage. Black smoke veiling the skeleton. Running, running, running...

Tad awakened with a start as the dream had been so vivid. He was wet with perspiration and couldn't go back to sleep, but the past kept going over and over in his mind.

It had been a close call, but he remembered joking about it as he stepped from his fur coat and leather pants. Bragging that he hadn't crashed on German soil.

Several weeks later, he reached his camp, weary of the war and with a fear of flying he had never felt before. To fight the fear, between missions, he found solace in the bars. Drowning in the sparkling red of the wine and embers of brandy. Making love to the

French girls, dark eyes, desirable bodies. Flying the next day became tolerable.

Then he had met Renee Deval, more slender than most of the other French girls. Huge dark eyes that seemed much too big for the petite face. He twirled the glass of brandy in his hand watching as a funnel formed in the liquid, reflecting the figure of a dancer just budding into womanhood. She had begged for cigarettes, but he laughed, handing her a piece of chocolate. And she had cried. Later they had walked together and he had told her about his Grandfather Silas, about Oregon where apples grew big and round and red. Language had been a barrier, but her eyes teased and her lips promised as they made love under the stars, almost under the eyes of her parents.

Then as if to end a bad nightmare, the war ended. Love had made them one, but a year would have to pass before she could join him in America. As his ship sailed back to America, he watched from the deck, glimpsing a French girl in a white dress waving goodbye.

A year later, Tad read the words of Emma Lazarus to Renee, as they stood beneath the three hundred and five feet tall Statue of Liberty.

Give me your tired, your poor,

Your huddled masses yearning to breathe free, The wretched refuse of your teeming shore, Send these, the homeless, tempest-tost to me, I lift my lamp beside the golden door.

For six years, they shared an ideal union. Davie was born less than a year following their marriage. When Davie was five years old, they were expecting another child. But the child was not born. Renee complained of an uneasiness, a weariness; they blamed it on the pregnancy. Two months before the child was due, Renee died; influenza, the doctor said.

To Tad, the grief was unbearable and he sought comfort in the bottle. When he lost his job, he wrote his brother Matthew and boarded the train for Oregon.

From France to New York to Oregon, the Wright's homestead, bees droning in the old pear tree. *Life is like a beehive,* he thought, *a high-pitched happiness and a deep, deep sadness. Then there is nothing at all.*

"I'm not going to stay," Davie said, bringing Tad back to the present. They were at the Portland train station, and through the window, Tad saw Matthew and Susan.

"I'm not staying with you," Davie repeated as Susan reached for him. "Only until Daddy comes to get me."

"I'm not going to stay," Davie said again, eyeing Susan suspiciously.

Susan clasped the child's hand tightly. "Of course."

Chapter 21
Great Grandfathers Tree of Life

*P*ortland was an easy place to sit and drink until every memory was dimmed. Tad lost one job after another. He pulled lumber off the green chain in a sawmill, worked at the ships' docks, and then he worked in another mill. Finally, he had no steady occupation. Sometimes, he would work a day or two until he had enough money for whiskey. Then he drank until his money ran out and found another job.

He did not know how he got to bed at night. Sometimes, he would wake up in a flophouse, sometimes sprawled across a bed in a room he did not remember entering. Bars, women, joints. When he tried to stop drinking, his days were nightmares, but the nights were hell.

"Guess what? Uncle Matt has a pony for you."

Davie's eyes widened. "A pony!" He was sure now that he would like Aunt Susan. He didn't know about Uncle Matt.

The pear tree was fragrant with flowers, and the bees were flying from flower to flower, when they reached the farm. Tad had seen it in his memory over and over again. He was home, but he felt a chill, and he clung to his child.

"Son," he said, "this is your great-grandfather's tree of life."

Davie looked at the tree. It looked just like any other tree, only it was bigger. It was the bees that fascinated him.

Matthew looked at Susan. Her face was beaming with happiness and she was looking at Tad. Matthew pushed his chair back from the table.

"Show Tad and David to their room, Susan," he said. "I've got some stumps to dig before dark." He left to harness his team, but neither Susan nor Tad raised their eyes to watch him go.

The next afternoon, Tad left for Portland.

It was another six months before Tad visited Matthew and Susan again. Davie ran out to meet him as he stepped out of the car. He had not missed his father nearly as much as he anticipated.

"Hello, Dad!" he called, seeming much older than the little boy Tad had left in Susan's care. He hugged his father a moment, then with a happy squeal, he ran to play.

Alone with Susan, Tad could not deny that the sight of her stirred him. She was young and vibrant. Golden hair framed a small freckled face. Her smooth arms were sprinkled with small, lighter-toned freckles, lighter because of the long sleeves, she so often wore. She looked as young as she had the first time he kissed her before he had gone to France. He placed his arm around her waist. "Susan, you're looking good!"

"Tell me about your job," Susan asked excitedly. "Do you like it?"

The entrancement faded at the sound of Matthew's wagon on the gravel. Tad quickly released Susan, and Susan flushed as she mopped a strand of hair back from her moist forehead.

The next morning, Matthew had already left the house to work in the fields. When Tad and Susan were sitting across the breakfast table, Tad asked, "How is it that you and Matthew never had a child?"

Susan raised her eyes self-consciously to his. The question had been abrupt.

"I don't know," she said simply.

Tad recalled his mother saying that Matthew had the mumps when he was fourteen and it was doubtful he could ever be a father. His mother had believed in all sorts of old wives' tales; now he wondered if there was any truth in the old theory about having mumps go down on a male, causing sterility. There was a look of despair on Susan's face, and he wished he had not asked the question.

The weekend was almost over, and Tad prepared to go back to Portland, promising David he would see him in another month.

There was a dragon with a fiery tongue and horny scales, slithering in and out of the tiny knothole in the ceiling.

For a while, it had looked small, like a lizard he had watched when he was a boy. It fell from the ceiling and coiled over Davie and around him, crushing his chest, wrapping itself around his body. He could feel its icy breath on his bare flesh.

He screamed and screamed.

When he awakened, he was in the big bedroom of his childhood, only it was Matthew's home now. Roses bloomed in red and yellow on the wallpaper. His arms and legs were held fast and he could not move. Then he was lost again in a flaming pit. The bees swarmed and flew away from the pear tree. They crawled over his decomposed body, devouring him.

He was dead, but he still felt pain. He wept in his torment, and when he stopped weeping, Susan was there, Susan, with dark circles around her eyes. He laid his head on her breast and wept.

"Matt's gone!" she said. "I had to tell him."

"Susan." He shook her until her eyes looked haunted with disbelief. "What did you tell him?"

She turned her face away. "We quarreled. I had to spend so much time with you when Matthew brought you from Portland, you were like a crazy man. Tad, someone had to watch you."

She started to rise from his bed where she had been sitting. He seized her hands and drew her down again roughly. "What did you tell him?"

"I told him I didn't love him, that I married him when I was still in love with you. I told him. Oh, God! Is it wrong to love someone so much?"

"But he's my brother, my own brother."

The doctor came the next day and left sedatives. For days, Tad was in a semi-stupor. Susan kept a vigilance beside his bedside, waiting for him to stir.

"Tad," she wept, "you can't drink anymore. Alcohol is poison to you. Tad, the doctor said you'll die if you don't quit."

"Die?" he said. "I'm already dead."

Then Matthew came. Matthew the sullen, Matthew the wronged, Matthew his brother. A look of hatred burned his eyes. "I could kill you," he said, "but I'll let whiskey do it for me."

"Matt, please hear me out," Tad pleaded. "It's not true. Susan was upset. There's nothing between us, I swear to God!"

"Nothing between you? Susan expecting and there's nothing between you? Tad, you're a drunken bastard. You come to my home and you sleep with my wife. Then you tell me there's nothing between you."

"Susan expecting? You're her husband. How can you hang something like that on me?"

"You know damn well I'm sterile."

"Matt, have you ever been to a doctor? You're just as bad as Ma, believing those old wives' tales. There never was a thing between me and Susan. Sure, I kissed her once, just once. When she was just a kid. I kissed all the girls that night. It was a wild party. I was going away."

"And I'm supposed to believe that? Susan's been mooning around over you ever since you brought your kid here."

"Don't be a fool, Matt. I'll get out of here. I'll go back East."

"I hope you roast in hell!" Matthew slammed the door.

Susan was peeling potatoes and looked up guiltily when Tad came into the kitchen.

"Susan," Tad said gently, "is it true what Matt said?"

"I thought I was to blame," Susan said, sobbing. "Why didn't he tell me? I could have helped him. I would have understood."

"But why didn't you tell me?"

"I didn't plan it. I want you to know that. You were so sick, sometimes you were out of your head and said things, and you cried. I had never heard a man cry. It was awful. You'd cry yourself to sleep in my arms. Matthew worked so hard. We were by ourselves and it happened. Please don't hate me, Tad. I couldn't help it. I loved you."

Tad held her close. "I don't hate you, Susan. I'm no damn good, you know that?"

She kissed his lips. "You're kind and gentle. You make me feel like a woman. Matthew isn't like you. I don't matter to him. Sometimes, I think he married me just to have someone to cook for him."

The new baby was christened Harry. David was seven years old, but it wasn't clear to him. Uncle Matthew had gone away this time, but his father stayed. And Aunt Susan had become his mother, and he had a new brother.

A sin such as Tad's and Susan's was not easy to hide from the small community, but time passed and the neighbors seemed to forget the gossip.

Months passed—spring, summer, and fall. Apples were picked, sorted, and hand-packed into barrels to be shipped to all points of the world. A letter arrived from Matthew. He had remarried and was logging in Alaska. If all went well, he'd make a visit with his new family the following year.

The old collie barked a welcome and wagged his tail as a stranger walked toward the house. A small dark-haired woman walked a few steps behind him. It was Matthew. Susan retired to the background, shading her eyes from the sun. Tad ran to meet him, embracing his brother, the hatred forgiven.

"I had to go north to find Amy," Matthew said proudly. "And what's more, a ready-made family." He called to the three anxious children waiting in the car. "Get out, kids!"

Matthew's three children stood fascinated at the foot of the pear tree, watching the activity of the bees. David sat watching the children but did not join them. When they went into the house, he stayed behind.

The grass beneath the pear tree was damp with the evening dew, and the bees swarmed around him. David did not move.

Is life always like this? he wondered. *Happiness and sadness. Daddy and Uncle Matthew friends again. Mama was sick and Mama died. Daddy screamed. Uncle Matthew got mad and ran away.*

David took a stick and dug into the ground, scattering the dirt around him. Guess some days are happy, but most of them are sad.

"Come, son," his father called.

David shook his head. "I want to dig some more," he said. He dug a big hole in the ground, making it deep enough to hold the dead squirrel. When he laid it in the ground, he saw the blood on its head where his 22 bullet had hit it.

Dying, he thought, *means rotting in the ground. Mama died.* With his foot, he pushed the dirt over the squirrel. He piled the dirt into a mound, then he stuck the stick into the earth to mark the grave.

Part IV
The Larsons

Chapter **22**

In Northwestern Missouri

*L*og houses, ghostly inhabited by rats and ground squirrels, sunk back into the earth from which they sprang as brush and wild vines climbed over the walls. Doors creaked as the wind caught the rotted boards and rusty hinges, sending a chill through those who passed by, remembering and envying the brave ones. Those who had the courage to leave. For miles up and down the river, small farms lay decrepit and unfruitful by those who dared defy the river, its spring upheaval railing the topsoil and carrying it away, carving a new route through the land. As the river gnawed away at the soil, more and more family ties were broken. Many were joining the wagon train at Trenton and heading westward in search of new land.

Andrew Larson slumped on the bar stool, drinking his whiskey straight as he listened to the talk of the journey.

He shared the unrest; for three years, he had faced the frustration of the spring floods and summer droughts. Three years in which there was no seed to sow and none to harvest. One late spring followed another; planting was put off so that when fall came, immature grain bent under autumn winds and the crop had to be plowed under; corn rotted in the ground; seedlings drowned in a sea of water or if they survived the flooding, scorched as the hot summer sun baked the tender shoots.

Cruel years that tried the farmers as they watched their livestock grow thin and market prices fall. It was as if the land that stretched along the river was cursed.

Andrew drank another shot of whiskey, then stopped momentarily to gather more information about the journey. He was young and strong and had made up his mind. He was willing to leave the damned land to the river and the sun; he was going west.

The early May evening was crisp, remembering winter, anticipating summer. As Andrew approached the shanty, he could see his wife Elizabeth through the open door. The dim light of the candle resting gently on her tear-stained face. Elizabeth was not quite right in the head. She had almost died of typhoid, and at times, her mind clouded. It disturbed him that she would leave the door open when he was away.

For days, she would be as sane as he was, then something would come over her, and he would find her sitting alone, her eyes vacant and staring. These times, he treated her as a child, for her mind then was as innocent as a child's.

Elizabeth was kneeling near her trunk. Andrew watched as she took two small christening gowns from the trunk. She fondled them for a few moments, then folded them gently and returned them to their hiding place. *Women are sentimental,* he thought.

"Bets," he spoke her name gently.

She raised her face when he spoke her name.

"We're going, aren't we, Andrew?" she asked, tears forming on her lashes.

She turned from him and brushed the tears away.

"Bets," he put his arms around her and held her to him.

"Are we doing the right thing? I could find work in Jefferson City, and we could be near the children."

He had said it. Elizabeth did not move for a moment, then she walked away from him and stirred at the embers in the fireplace.

"Andrew," she said, still not looking at him. "I know it's hard on you, too. When things are good, we can send for them. They will be good, won't they?"

He kissed her gently, smoothing back the hair from her temples. "They will be good. I've got a feeling about it."

The whiskey had loosened his tongue, and he wanted to say many things he had kept from Elizabeth. "Bets, I need you so much. When you had the fever, I almost lost my mind. We can start over again. I heard so many things about Oregon.

Free land, we can build a log cabin and grow our own vegetables. The timber off the land is ours."

He wanted everything to be new, and he wanted a clear conscience most of all. "I've got to tell you, I haven't always been—"

Elizabeth put her finger over his mouth. "Shh, you don't have to tell me now or ever. If you've asked God for forgiveness, you have mine."

At that moment, Elizabeth felt very much a woman. She did not want to ever feel the hurt again she felt when she heard that Andrew had been going into town to see her cousin Lucy. *He feels guilty, that's all I want to know. He can't help himself, he's big and strong and needs a woman to make him feel warm and loved. I was sick with the fever, and I was carrying the children, and sometimes, I'm sorta wretched.*

Her emotions were strong; she wanted to possess him.

To be woman enough to shut out all of his thoughts of Lucy.

But when she came to him that night, he lay heavy on his back, weariness etched on his face. She lay next to him, hearing his steady breathing and feeling the stubble on his face. Her heart pounded and her head was swimming, but she would not awaken him. It was awhile before she too slept, and when she slept, her dreams went wild.

She was searching, searching like a madwoman, but she couldn't find them. Eric and little Peter, her babies, were gone.

The end of the month was nearing and the children were taken to Jefferson City. Tears did not flow. Peter and Eric had spent so much time with their grandparents when their mother was ill, that to them, Jefferson City was a second home. Two small faces pressed against the windowpane, watching as the wagon lurched away. It never occurred to their young minds that in time, this too would be but a memory.

Chapter 23
Their Journey

There was much gaiety at the start of the journey from Trenton. The early morning sun flooded the line of wagons with warmth and light. The wagons were freshly greased, the riggings solid, the canvas canopies new or expertly patched. There was laughter and singing as the wheels dug in and the tall prairie grasses swished the flanks of the horses and oxen to be trampled down by the following wagons until the trail was smooth.

After the third week, joy subsided. The sun was hot and enervating. Sweat rolled from man and beast. The women's hair was damp and lank and their clothing clung to them. The men stripped off their shirts, wiping their hairy chests and faces with the wet garment. The children were restless, the animals slow, and the dogs that had frisked behind the wagons jumped aboard, their tongues lolling. Still, they went on, stopping only to rest the burdened horses and oxen or to raise a wagon that had slipped off the trail and bogged down.

Months passed and the weary travelers were subjected to varying conditions. The hard pull of the wagon over wet ground, when the wheels sank axle-deep in mud, the jogging pace over hard-baked soil with the sun like a burning furnace, then rain in a steady stream that left a sea of mud.

There were thunder and lightning storms and winds that whipped and tore the canvas. Once, a lightning-felled tree blocked their passage. At night, there would be the cry of a sick child, the scream of a hysterical woman, and men cursing.

Meanwhile, Elizabeth guarded her secret. Before she left, she had felt certain that she was in the family way. *Forgive me, God,* she silently prayed. *I couldn't tell Andrew. Send your angels to care for Eric and little Peter, and bless this little one beneath my breast.*

It was mid-September and the end of the journey was nowhere in sight. There were unforeseen perils everywhere. Raging rivers that had to be spanned, breakdowns, hordes of insects. Once an ox stumbled into a gopher hole, broke a leg, and had to be put out of its misery.

Later, when they placed a small white cross above the grave of a child, Elizabeth clung to Andrew.

"Thank God," she said, "that we were unselfish enough to leave the children with Mother." But in the nighttime, when everyone was asleep, Elizabeth would open the trunk and fondle the little dresses.

She lay next to Andrew when he felt the quickening.

"Oh, Lord, why didn't you tell me?" he cried. "What if I lose you too?"

She held him close and stroked his cheek. "I couldn't, Andrew. You'd have thought of me and either gone alone or not at all. We had to make the change. God must have wanted it that way."

"God! How can you mention God? Look at me, Elizabeth. God wanted this?"

She looked at him, at the hollow eyes and lean body. Yet his muscles were hard.

"Look at these people," he said. "Half of them don't have the slightest idea what is going to happen to them. Do you think we'll all make it? For God's sake, Elizabeth, this is Indian country. The train ahead of us some of them...my God..."

Elizabeth paled. The baby stirred and darkness engulfed her, but she faced straight ahead and stiffened the stubborn look of her German father on her face.

"We'll make it, Andrew," she whispered. "We'll pray. Do you remember how you used to praise God when things went right? We need His help!"

That night, her baby was born—born and died without a breath or a whimper. Andrew wept openly as he placed the small form in a pine box and marked the grave with a cross made from an oxen bow, and Elizabeth comforted him, neglecting the release her own tears could have furnished her.

When the wagons started to move out, she took the reins from Andrew's hand.

"Just you sit easy now," she ordered. Andrew pulled the big hat down over his eyes and stretched his long legs. The wagon bounced and churned over the rocky trail, and Andrew put his hope in Elizabeth's God for he knew that it was only her faith which had taken them this far.

It was mid-November, snow in the mountains delayed them, but the dry leaves crunched under the wagon wheels. The wagon train halted on a knoll that overlooked the valley, still, cool, and green as an emerald, nestling between snowcapped mountains. Tall fir trees soared toward the sky and were mirrored in the shimmering waters of the Willamette.

The misty steady rains had begun, clearing the dust from the air. It fell on their faces, a gift from heaven.

They had reached their destination. The one-hundred-sixty-acre homestead lay only a week's journey over the pass.

The land was virgin and reluctant to be taken. But timber was felled, deep roots were blasted out, and the rich earth was plowed and harrowed. Andrew Larson cleared ten acres, groomed the logs, and split the shakes that roofed the crude hut. Then he planted his first crop.

The first few years were lean, but Elizabeth busied herself in the kitchen. She salted down the winter's meat and preserved the wild blackberry and worked hand and hand with Andrew in the fields. During the six years that followed, there were other children. All girls. When she held them in her arms, she remembered two other children, but only in the night did she weep for her sons, when her daughters were lost to an influenza epidemic. She only had her sons to weep for.

Andrew Larson loved the West. He loved the vast expanse of land, the fertile soil, the cold clear streams, and as he scanned the tall timber, he dreamed of the day when he would own the land as far as his eyes could see and yonder over the mountain.

He built a crude sawmill. From dawn to dusk, he felled the fir, trimmed the branches, then hand-sawed the logs into proper lengths. He pushed the logs through crude machinery until the sweetness of sliced lumber filled his nostrils and the sawdust got into his shoes and clung to his hair.

He cursed the horses that pulled the chained logs out of the gullies and pushed and pulled with his own strength until his muscles ached.

The crude mill was mechanized, and he hired men, and he bought more timber to feed the hungry saws that cut and sliced with amazing swiftness. He bought more land and the trees that grew on other land until the mill moaned and buzzed from daylight until dark.

The lumber was packed in square piles held together by steel bands and shipped to distant points. It became a never-ending process because the land was covered with trees. And when the land was cleared, ranches spread across the valley. Large homes were built, large families were raised, orchards and nut trees were planted, and as the men came, more women came. With the women came beauty. Roses were cultivated, imported

Dutch bulbs were planted, and soon there were cities and colleges.

Andrew Larson had accomplished much in those years.

The home he had planned for Elizabeth was built; his day-dreams became a reality.

Months became years. For twenty years, he had labored, and in those twenty years, he had not seen his mother or father and he had not mourned for his sons.

Then, as if to arrest his frenzied pace, there came a hot and cloudless summer. The woods were closed to men and machinery for fear of starting a forest fire. Without the constant supply of logs to feed it, the sawmill closed down.

The men were restless, and days became weeks and then a month.

Early in August, a telegram arrived. Andrew's mother was ill. When he boarded the train in Portland, he realized that he had not kissed Elizabeth goodbye and that they had not shared the bed for several weeks. This tormented him. He thought of the sons he would soon see again. *Darling Elizabeth,* he thought, *I can never make up for the years I've deprived you of your boys.* He had kept his word and remained faithful to her during his years in the

West. Now he wondered which was the greater sin: committing adultery or taking a mother from her children.

As the train sped over the land they had traveled by wagon, he viewed the timber. *Timber,* he thought, *I've become lost in industry. I scarcely see Elizabeth and the girls. I have thought only of my mills and of Andrew Larson.*

As the smokestacks of the city loomed over the horizon, a weary man emerged from the train. Andrew Larson at forty-seven had built himself an empire, a monster that consumed his every moment.

His father, Lars, met him at the door.

"She's gone," he said slowly.

"Oh, no!" Andrew said. There was nothing else he could say. He had wanted to see her alive one more time, but that would never be.

"It's a blessing she went," his father added. "She had a stroke. I didn't write because I didn't want you to worry." His father still spoke with a Scandinavian accent. How could he tell his son that Catherine no longer thought of him as her son?

Andrew felt the estrangement. His mother had been ill, and he had been too busy even to ask about her health.

He should have known that time could not stand still.

"The boys, they've been lots of help." The old man's eyes glowed as he spoke of them. "Eric is just like you, and Peter, he's a smart one. He's studying law. I s'pose you're wanting them with you now."

Andrew looked at his father, trying to soften his words. "Yes, Dad. Elizabeth would like to see them. I owe that much to her."

"Ya, I s'pose so."

Andrew wanted to escape. Flee from the past that was engulfing him in memories, obliterating the present. His mother's chair, the spinning wheel where wool had been twisted and pulled into yarn. He walked into the backyard: the petunia beds, the stoned walk, the fishing pond, trees.

The funeral was at the church. The same church he had attended as a child, christened, married, and where his sons were christened. Now, the same church that held his happiest memories was the scene of his deepest grief. The grief that lodges in the pit of your stomach and gnaws at your very soul, grief that sinks deeper and deeper until you want to die, then suddenly it goes away.

Andrew took one last look at his mother's wasted body. Regrets nagged him, and he wanted to curse the years that had drifted by. Letters never written, thoughts never expressed, and the money he had neglected to send for his sons' education. But the tears would not flow; there was no relief from the gnawing pain. *Where is Elizabeth's just God?* he questioned silently.

Eric sobbed openly and Andrew tried to comfort his son. From out of the corner of his eye, he could see his other son, Peter, sitting erect and rigid in the pew. Peter sat dry-eyed.

Outside in the churchyard cemetery, the sun beat unmercifully upon the mourners. Andrew watched as the coffin was lowered into the ground. Perspiration dripped from his brow and the emptiness inside of him was almost unbearable. Lord, he wanted to go home. He ached for Elizabeth, longing for arms to hold him so he could weep. Most of all, he wanted to lie close to her and sleep, if he ever slept again.

After the funeral services were over, Andrew was anxious for his journey home. The carpenters' trade was slow and Eric had agreed to accompany his father. Peter was not interested, and as Andrew prepared to leave, he approached Peter.

Peter was on the porch reading.

"Have you any plans about your own practice?" Andrew asked. "I could, perhaps you could, Oregon's a new frontier and law is a good profession. I would like you to be near your mother. She misses you."

Peter stood up, slamming his book down on the handmade bench. "I'll choose my own location. I don't know you or my mother. Grandma was the only mother I ever knew." He picked up his book and walked into the house, leaving Andrew aghast with disbelief.

My son? he thought, questioning the relationship. *How else can it be? Twenty years ago, I left him here. I did not think Elizabeth could care for the children properly, I didn't trust her. There was work, and I didn't have money for the fare to send for them. Later, I had money, but I became lost in timber. I used the money to buy more timber. Now all the money in the world can't buy back my son's love.*

Chapter 24

Homecoming for the family

The yellow rose had climbed higher on the gate, and the apple trees were burdened with ripening fruit when Andrew and Eric returned to the valley. The pear tree which Silas Wright had planted was bearing a heavy crop, and Andrew's bees had escaped from their hive and were hanging in a big black cluster in the young tree.

Elizabeth and his daughters were waiting by the gate as they arrived.

"Bets," he said, using the endearment of long ago. "It's so good to be home." He held her at arm's length, searching her eyes for the love he had missed so much when he was gone, Eric standing like a stranger in the background.

Elizabeth raised her eyes slowly to look at her son. Tears rolled down her lashes unto her cheeks.

"Mama," Eric said gently as if remembering.

"Eric, my little boy, my baby." Elizabeth dried her tears away with her apron.

As he strolled about, time seemed to stand still, as if he had run straight into a mirror, reflecting himself as he had been twenty years ago.

"Eric!" his father had said. "Just like you." Father and son fell unabashed into each other's arms, then embarrassed by the display of emotion, stiffly shook hands.

Peter, his elder son, stood in the distance. His eyes were cold, appraising, and condemning. The lawyer, Andrew thought, flushing under the scrutiny. Andrew immediately thought of Elizabeth's father, large and overpowering. Now he suffered the same diminishment under the appraising gaze of his own son.

Dignified and composed, Peter approached his father.

"How are you, sir? I'm sorry we could not have met under less grueling circumstances." He spoke as if his own father was a complete stranger.

"I'm sorry too," Andrew said, trying to seem reserved, feeling unworthy of his son's attention.

"I'm studying law in St. Louis. Hope to set up my own practice."

"You'll make a good lawyer," Andrew said, sure of his statement. For this was a man that could tear the truth from you and that truth could tear you up inside until you felt like nothing at all.

"It was right for Peter to stay with Grandpa," she added. But from that time on, Elizabeth's eyes were sad. She still longed for her firstborn. That void was not filled with Eric's arrival. The years that separated them had become a gulf. She could only remember the child, and he could only visualize her as his mother.

Letters from Peter were infrequent; a printed invitation to his graduation exercises, a formal card announcing the opening of his office, a news clipping telling of his engagement, and after that, nothing at all.

Years slipped by, and the time came when he visited the mills only occasionally. Eric had taken his place well and was motivated by the same desire to modernize and expand.

Andrew could not break the habit of rising early, but now he sat in the sun or strolled about the vast lawn.

Elizabeth never mentioned her older son. Surely, Andrew thought, she must be accustomed to the loss.

But one morning, Andrew awakened to find Elizabeth's place in the bed empty. He searched for her and found her kneeling by the old trunk. She had removed the little christening dresses and was humming an old German lullaby, swaying with the tune, and he saw that her eyes were vacant and staring. He slipped away without disturbing her.

Chapter 25

Some going to their Heavenly Home

By afternoon, Elizabeth had returned to God. Andrew held her close, running his fingers through her hair. "Bets," he pleaded. "Forgive me. God forgive me." For the last time, he held her close, cherishing the moment which would have to last forever. Emotion throbbed through his body, and the tears came.

Three weeks later, Andrew Larson followed Elizabeth to eternal rest. He was tired, he said, so tired he could not go on without her, and Eric could carry on, but he died with Peter's name on his lips.

And the memory of Andrew Larson faded into the pages of Willamette Valley History; downy flakes of snow were falling in a town in Eastern Oregon. Judge Peter Larson drew the draperies aside to watch as the close-clipped courthouse lawn was blanketed. First, the snow had been wet and sticky; now it fell fluffy, tumbling from the sky, clinging to the shrubbery, one flake piling on another until one wondered how the branches could support the weight.

One large tree stood on the lawn, thick-trunked, scrawny branches bending in every direction. A snowbird flew from the ground and perched on a branch. The branch swayed and the bird flew away.

The judge took off his overcoat and lay it back down in the chair, realizing he still wore his robe. The day was over, as was his life; he was retiring from the bench. In his black cloak, he had seemed to many a stern, stone-faced mediator, holding the scales of justice in even balance. The younger lawyers viewed his judgment with respect and awe.

Here was a man that abided strictly by the law book, never known to sway in either direction until all the facts had been presented and weighed.

But the judge who was hanging up his vestment or mantle for the last time and running his fingers caressingly over the law books that lined the study had not always been the unstained advocate of justice. Peter Larson wore two hats.

There was Judge Larson the dignitary, and there was Peter Larson the man.

For the old judge, retirement did not mean a release from his judicial duties, but a termination. He had no future apart from the courtroom, and for him, there would be no tomorrows. His hair was snow-white, his eyes steel-blue and piercing. His mind was sharp and analytical still, but his body had grown weak and weary with the years.

So the old judge lingered, trying to muster strength to envision the days ahead, to dream of the future. But when there is no vision, dreams cease.

On the day that a man looks backward, retracing footsteps and forgetting the journey that still lies ahead, he is old. Memories of the past are suddenly fitted with gossamer wings and they flutter before the mind's eye until the past lives again.

The five senses evoke the scenes of the past and the present is forgotten. The regrets and mistakes are magnified and reality fades.

Recollections from the past! Two tiny faces pressed against a window watching a wagon rumble until it faded from sight. On many nights, he was awakened by his own agonized screams. An avalanche of snow was churning furiously down the mountain. It had engulfed his parents and sent their broken bodies hurtling into the valley below. Then the snow lay still and beautiful again, shimmering in the moonlight.

The letters that were read to him did not verify his childish nightmares. They had reached Oregon and would send for them soon, but to Peter, it had seemed safer to think of them as completely annihilated.

"Petie, is Mama coming soon?" Eric had asked him in childish anticipation.

Being older and much wiser, Peter had replied, "Naw, Oregon is a long ways, it ain't likely she will."

As time passes, the mind classifies the happiness and the sorrows of life and files them neatly away. The happy moments, often recalled, bring a ray of sunshine and lighten the burdens of living. The painful experiences remain hidden deep in the subconscious, then loom suddenly into importance.

The early April mornings were brisk, and the boy Peter shuffled along, kicking the dust with his feet. Some mornings he pranced, inhaling the cool air until he was exhausted.

The buds on the trees had started to swell, and here and there, in a protected spot, a new leaf trembled in the breeze. On days such as this, he sauntered on the path, whistling and listening as the birds answered. The flat stone held between his fingers felt slippery. He studied it a moment before he sailed it through the air, then watched it skip across the water, making a series of diminishing rings. The sun was rising higher. He had tarried, and now he must hasten his footsteps and take the short cut.

Peter walked swiftly past the row of tar-papered shacks that housed the Negro tenants of the Carsted Plantation. His heart beat fast and he wanted to run, yet he was curious too.

As he neared the makeshift settlement, he heard the sound of children at play, drowning out the gurgling of the creek and the song of the bird. He crept closer and closer until he could see the lines in old Lilly's face. She was a legend—a hundred years old, they said. Frizzled white hair framed a face eroded by life and age. He was so close that he could see the stark white of her eyes. They said she had been a slave all of her life; she was freed but had stayed on. A slave, the word lingered in his mind until tears stung his eyes and his vision blurred.

The shouts of the other children on their way to school aroused him. The children were throwing rocks at him and yelling, "Nigger lover! Peter's a nigger lover."

Blood rushed to his face and anger engulfed him. He flung his weight against the larger of the boys.

"Poor white trash! Poor white trash!" he screamed until his lungs were exhausted. He pounded the boy with his fists until he could not lift his arm for another blow.

Peter's nose was bleeding and his upper lip was gashed. Overhead, a small bird twittered, and Peter wept. It was an agony, not for the pain he felt, but for the pain for a people estranged because of the color of their skin.

"Git up!" Peter looked into the face of a giant of a man, and the face was black. "You all better be gitten les yer daddy whale the daylights out of you!"

The black man put out his big hand and helped Peter to his feet. He took a large red handkerchief, dipped it into the stream, and wiped the blood from the boy's face. "Now git!"

For a moment, Peter met the black man's gaze. Then he ran— Lord, how he ran—straight home, forgetting it was a school day.

Catherine Larson held Peter close. She did not understand.

"I'm not a nigger lover. I'm not!" Peter cried.

She stroked the hair back from the bruises on his face. "No, Peter. The blacks are God's people too. It's not a bad thing to be black, only some white folk think it is so."

In broken English, his grandmother tried to explain that they were a free people now, entitled to the rights of all Americans.

From that day on, Peter studied the life of Abraham Lincoln. Slavery had been abolished by law, but it still existed in the mind of the white man. It still existed in the black man. There was a gulf between the white and the black. Peter debated the statement that "all men were created equal." Actually, the poor whites were a little less than the Larsons and the blacks a little less than the poor whites. Where the dividing line was Peter did not know, but he knew that there was a division.

There were class distinctions between the rich and the poor, between the Jew and the Protestant, between royalty and commoners, between the ways of the old country and the new, between each generation.

The old judge was weary now, for living in the past takes its toll of emotions, but for Peter Larson to tear himself away from past memories was impossible. His whole life had been devoted to the study of law. He was sworn to uphold justice, but the very things he had once condemned he had to condone. As a lawyer, he was no longer a free man with moral convictions. He was a public servant, a defender of human passions and corruptions. To win a case, he would defend unto death his client whether the client was innocent or guilty.

"Woe unto you, lawyers! For ye have taken away the key of knowledges ye entered not in yourselves, and them that were entering in ye hindered."

If man were put on earth to learn by trial and error, Peter Larson had not cooperated in the plan. He took on the guilt of the condemned. For a price, he had often been the defender of the guilty rather than of the guiltless. Soon, he had the reputation of being the most promising criminal attorney in the Midwest. With this came the strategy of power and politics.

Chapter 26

Judge Larson reviews his life

As Judge Larson continued to review his life, he saw again Marie Chapman, tall, beautiful, and spoiled, the daughter of a prominent St. Louis politician. Marie had her eye on Peter Larson. They had met on several formal occasions while he was still an unknown lawyer. She had not then seemed aware of his youth and handsomeness. However, as he lifted his sights and soared to political office, Marie saw him from a new angle.

Peter was aware that Marie was watching him. He had met those calculating eyes over a glass of champagne. Only when he felt her fingers touch his sleeve did he dare hope he was being seduced.

"Peter Larson, Father told me you were a most promising young attorney. He did not *say* that you were also daring and handsome."

Peter felt the blood rush to his face. He raised his eyes to hers only to find that they were as steady as his.

It was he who turned away, he who had the ability to sum up a person at one glance.

The perfume she wore made him heady, and he arose and went to her. Without thought of the outcome, he gripped her upper arm and escorted her to the dance floor. He was an expert orator in the courtroom; now he found himself tongue tied.

Their bodies entwined as they danced.

"There seem to be a lot of things my father did not tell me," she said when she had regained her composure. "He didn't tell me that you are a very persuasive young man."

Peter gulped. "I'm sorry I rushed you. It's just that I felt like a goldfish out of water standing there."

They returned to their table.

"Peter," she said softly. "May I call you Peter?"
"If I may call you Marie."

"Marie and Peter," she mused, her eyes intent on his. "They sound lovely together. Don't you agree?"

Peter raised his glass to hers. "To Marie, the girl I plan to make my wife."

The statement did not shock her. She raised her glass and touched it with her lips. "You are sure of yourself, aren't you?"

Blue eyes feasted on blue eyes.

"Yes," he said.

It was the only proposal or attempt at one that Peter made to Marie. From that evening on, Marie was Peter's betrothed. With her as his wife, the status climb up the ladder of success was not so steep. Years later, Peter realized that the thorns of a loveless marriage were a lot sharper than he had anticipated on the night when he had yielded so easily to an impulse.

"Marie," the name formed on the judge's lips. *I used her as a stepping-stone,* he thought, *Marie, spoiled child of luxury. I purchased the big house, I dressed her in fancy clothes. We entertained lavishly and she died having my child.* Perspiration beaded the old man's brow, and he pressed his handkerchief against it.

Fragments of court scenes dulled his vision, and justice appeared before him, the blindfold only covering one eye, the balance held firmly in her hands, the scales tipping toward the left side.

"My God!" he cried in anguish, for he knew that his mind was punishing him. It was like the recurring dream in which he had punished his parents for leaving him.

He had paid the penalty for his years of success, for his success had been tinged sometimes with the blood of the innocent. But it had been a success. Had he not sat for several weeks while a panel of his associates questioned, insulted, and hammered at him? Had he not emerged unstained? But the publicity had been too much for Marie. She had attempted to rid herself of his child and she had died.

He had not been disbarred, and when it was all over, had his success not been sweeter than before?

He had made a personal vow to God then. As a young lawyer, he had sold his soul for wealth and the lures of lust. He had vowed that if he was spared the humiliation of losing his practice, he would devote the remainder of his life to meting out justice—absolute justice.

It was then that he had remembered his father and had journeyed West. He had started over, right from the very bottom, and he had climbed again, straight as an arrow. Now there was no corruption. Peter Larson abided strictly by the law book *like* the laws were made by men.

Marie had been but a chapter of the past, and the vacancy she left was filled by Helen Watson. Helen was a waitress in the coffee shop of the hotel where he had taken a small room.

Helen Watson—short, matronly, unpolished—had little to offer Peter in the ways of political attainment. She was a reserved mature woman in whom Peter confided. He spent many evenings with her, delving deep into a summary which had caused him concern. In Peter's estimation, she was the physical side of his existence. A hotel waitress with little more than an eighth-grade education, she conformed to his estimation of the lower status, but he did not admit this even to himself.

He just never appeared with her in public. Peter Larson could not evaluate his need for her at night but was reluctant to be seen in her company in the presence of his peers.

Helen was his private life, his life away from the courtroom. Only yesterday, the old judge reminisced, Helen was laid away. A feeling of loss engulfed him, and he was solemn. It had been years since he had sought her company, and he was then a young judge.

He had had a strenuous day in court, a day when uncertainties clouded his decisions. He had imposed a sentence on a young Negro and later had wondered whether he would have been more lenient if the man had been white. There was no room for prejudice in the courtroom, but Peter Larson was a mere man, not God. The question had kept nagging him, and he had gone to Helen that night.

Helen was unusually quiet, and he could see that she had been crying. He was impatient with her. After all, his problems were vastly important; hers were insignificant. Then she told him she was carrying his child.

He walked over to the coal range that stood in the corner of the room. He calmly poured a cup of coffee and added his own whiskey.

"Marriage is out of the question," he said. "It's not that I don't love you." Love, he pondered that word, as he looked at her, love, the total acceptance of one person for another, a mutual agreement. But love, he thought, has spiritual as well as the physical values.

Two minds must meet on the same plane.

"Love," Helen interrupted his thoughts. "Is it love, or do you just need me?"

"I don't know, Helen. I've made many mistakes. I just don't know!"

"Is it a mistake to give your child a name?"

He noticed the premature gray in her hair, the weary lines around her eyes.

"Helen," he said simply, "we could go on just as always. I'll support you and the child, we are happy as we are."

"Happy?" she said, her voice husky. "Peter, do you doubt that this is your child?"

He set the coffee cup down on the table, and a hard line formed around his mouth. "It's the oldest trick in the world," he said. "And I'll be damned if I'll be roped in by it."

The color drained from Helen's face, and tears slid down her cheeks. "Is it because I don't have schooling?"

"It's something like that," he confessed. "Don't make me say it."

"You don't have to say it. I'm good enough in bed, but I'm not good enough to be your wife."

That was years ago, he thought. *I left her there without a twinge of conscience. I did not even stop at the bar. I walked to my room and went to bed. Any other man would have tossed and turned all night, but I slept like a baby.*

Each day I lived, I lived for myself. There was once Marie, and there was Helen. There could have been Marie's child, but it never had a chance. But I did have a child, he thought, *a daughter by Helen, and she was named Meredith.*

He remembered now the first time he had seen Meredith.

A gangly child of eight or nine, she had looked him straight in the eye, and he had wondered if Helen had told her about him. *No,* he thought, *she did not tell her.*

Years later, he had attended her high school graduation. He had sent her a check. He remembered the note he sent with the check. "Best wishes from a friend." *Friend,* he thought,

I was never a friend, not even to Helen. Now Meredith was a sophomore in college, a lovely woman, he thought. *I would be proud to claim her as my daughter, but it is too late.*

In his thoughts, he spanned the intervening years.

Summer had passed into fall, the autumn leaves had turned into a golden tan, then dried to a dead brown, crisp and weightless. The trees were shorn and naked and ugly. The winter winds blew cold each morning, snow fell in the foothills, and news of Helen's death reached the courthouse.

The screen on the front porch of the house where he had spent so many hours was still badly in need of repair.

He had planned to mend it but never had. The curtains had been checkered chintz; now they were of some heavier material.

Even the wallpaper had been changed, but Helen's touches were everywhere, the colorful braided rug in the hallway, the needlepoint, framed and hanging on the wall. He remembered the swiftness of her fingers as they drew the multicolored silks in and out.

Now the house smelled of death. The scent of the flowers surrounding the casket overwhelmed him. Helen's body lay in repose in the grotesque coffin, which reminded him of the way he had felt about the kitchen range in her house so long ago; it was overpowering in the demure room.

He strolled respectfully to the coffin to view her and saw a slight smile on her lips. Regrets and remorse overwhelmed him. He remembered his grandmother's funeral long ago. He had not cried then, and tears would not fall now. The tears choked him and he longed for their release, but they would not flow. He put his hand out and touched Helen's cold hands, remembering her smile, her laughter, her love—love, the word he feared to define.

Meredith entered the room. He looked upon his flesh and blood, and he removed his hat, feeling guilty that he had neglected to do so earlier out of respect for the dead.

"I came," he said, attempting an explanation, "to pay my last respects to your mother."

Her penetrating eyes looked into his. "You could have showed her some respect while she was still alive."

"You know?" he asked.

"She told me when she knew that she was going to die. I wish to God she had not."

"I was your mother's friend. We had a special sort of relationship."

"Special? She wasn't your cup of tea, was she? She wasn't sophisticated and pretty, she wasn't good enough for you. Am I good enough?"

"Meredith…" He put his hand out to touch her arm, but Meredith drew away.

"A man does strange things sometimes," he said. "I had a whole future ahead of me in law. Marriage seemed an impossibility, the talk, the scandal that follows things like this."

"She had to face all that alone because you didn't have the guts to do the right thing."

"I know I was wrong."

"Wrong!" she cried. Then, seeing her mother's face, she lowered her voice, turned to the door, and opened it.

"Good day, Judge Larson, it was kind of you to make this last visit."

"Meredith, I'll send a check to cover expenses. I'll see you through school."

"Your Honor," she said the words in bitter mockery, "I don't need your money."

The door shut, and he was out in the snow-covered street. The wind blew the new top snow into swirls against his overcoat and hat. The weight of his sick world bowed him down, and his gait was slow and unsteady. Suddenly, Judge Larson felt very, very old.

His office seemed dark and cold, for nowhere was there anyone as alone and burdened by guilt as he. The Honorable Judge Larson—accused, condemned, and convicted—by his own child.

The sun came out for a moment to shine on the snow, then clouds shut out the light. Peter Larson, guilty of every sin, redeemed only by the blood of Christ. The words were almost audible. He raised the gavel in his hand and let it fall heavily on the bench. It echoed throughout the empty courthouse.

There was a soft knock on the door, and he opened the door. The snow was still falling.

"Come in," he said. "Come in."

Meredith came into the room, her cheeks pink from the cold, snow clinging to her hair and clothing. "I've been walking and thinking. I don't know you well enough to call you Father, but Mother loved you and understood you."

Tears were falling now from the eyes of the young girl, from Peter Larson's eyes too.

"I can't live with hate," she said. "I wanted to hate you for what you did to my mother. I can't, Mother would want me to forgive you, she forgave you. I must tell you that."

"My child," Peter said, holding his daughter to him.

About Margaret
(Marjori) Wiese

Margaret was born as Margaret Ann Wicklund on November 17, 1925. She was born at home and was very small. She slept in a drawer with a hot water bottle that was covered to keep her warm. Even though she was small, she had a fighting Spirit within her that kept her alive. She was the second girl to be born to Gust and Alvina Wicklund. Born with black silky hair and dark brown eyes. Growing up, she had heart problems, but she grew to love her family, becoming a pal for her dad. She would go with her dad almost everywhere he went. Her mom would send her with him, because she was watching the other children. Margaret was happy to be with her dad. She loved to read for her pastime. She helped with chores given to her. She had dreams of someday going out West. She grew to be a beauty and had many boyfriends. It is funny that one boy saw her as a scrawny little girl. Then on a class reunion, he wanted to take her out, and she would not go out with him.

Then World War II came and Margaret wanted to do her part, so she became a nurse cadet. She also began working at a hospital in Minnesota. She started corresponding with the boys that were fighting for our freedom. One boy stood out and his name was Curtis Allen Wiese. Curtis was quite a jokester, and he would tell her that he had black hair and was short and fat. Margaret took her chances, and they met in Minneapolis where she lived at a boarding house with her sister. Margaret was pleasantly surprised to see a handsome blonde-haired, blue-eyed sailor at the door. It might not been love at first sight, but the interest was sure there, so they continued to correspond till the end of the war. They got married soon after. Even though Margaret was told she could not have any children, Margaret proved them wrong and had two boys and two girls.

With her love for writing, she wrote what came to her from poems to short stories to novels. She went to several publishers, sharing her work with them, also, sending them her manuscripts. Her daughter Tami sent them off for her. The postmaster got to know her and I am sure looked forward to her coming in. Margaret would get her inspirations from her surroundings, and *The Bee Tree* was born from her looking out the kitchen window at the pear tree with bees sucking the nectar out of the pears that fell on the ground. The bees seemed to get drunk from the nectar and brought an inspiration for a book that would be a favorite for the whole family.

Margene Wiese-Baier's view of The Bee Tree

My Mom came to me in a Dream and told me that she wanted me to publish her books. I argued with her in the dream and told her that I did not know how to publish her books and that I was not qualified, but to no avail she still insisted. I finally conceded and told her that I would get them published.

I was so excited to get her book Wymans Creek published. I didn't know I would be even more excited to get her book The Bee Tree published. I scanned the manuscript and started reading it and as I corrected and made sure all the words were in the writing from her typed papers. Even though I wanted to find a clean copy that was not to be. Even though Mom has been in Heaven since 1985 it was almost like she was sitting next to me helping me to get it done. Telling me Margene, you can do it. I believe in you.

I had put off doing her book until after finishing my two books, so I could concentrate fully on her book. I discovered that Mom writing The Bee Tree was and has been my inspiration to become a writer. I kept saying to myself. Mom you are really a wonderful writer. The Bee Tree is truly a dedication and inspired by Abba Father, Jesus and Holy Spirit.

I did not change any words that my Mom wrote, but just made sure everything she wrote was there for all to see and read for themselves.

Mom I am so proud of you for achieving your Dream even from Heaven. Love, your daughter Margene <3.